Food Trends and Prospects
in India

FRED H. SANDERSON
SHYAMAL ROY

Food Trends and Prospects in India

THE BROOKINGS INSTITUTION
Washington, D.C.

Library of Congress Cataloging in Publication Data:

Sanderson, Fred Hugo, 1914–
　Food trends and prospects in India.

　Includes bibliographical references and index.
　1. Food supply—India.　2. Agriculture—Economic
aspects—India.　I. Roy, Shyamal, joint author.
II. Title.
HD9016.I42S27　　338.1'9'54　　79-24391
ISBN 0-8157-7703-5

1 2 3 4 5 6 7 8 9

THE BROOKINGS INSTITUTION is an independent organization devoted to nonpartisan research, education, and publication in economics, government, foreign policy, and the social sciences generally. Its principal purposes are to aid in the development of sound public policies and to promote public understanding of issues of national importance.

The Institution was founded on December 8, 1927, to merge the activities of the Institute for Government Research, founded in 1916, the Institute of Economics, founded in 1922, and the Robert Brookings Graduate School of Economics and Government, founded in 1924.

The Board of Trustees is responsible for the general administration of the Institution, while the immediate direction of the policies, program, and staff is vested in the President, assisted by an advisory committee of the officers and staff. The by-laws of the Institution state: "It is the function of the Trustees to make possible the conduct of scientific research, and publication, under the most favorable conditions, and to safeguard the independence of the research staff in the pursuit of their studies and in the publication of the results of such studies. It is not a part of their function to determine, control, or influence the conduct of particular investigations or the conclusions reached."

The President bears final responsibility for the decision to publish a manuscript as a Brookings book. In reaching his judgment on the competence, accuracy, and objectivity of each study, the President is advised by the director of the appropriate research program and weighs the views of a panel of expert outside readers who report to him in confidence on the quality of the work. Publication of a work signifies that it is deemed a competent treatment worthy of public consideration but does not imply endorsement of conclusions or recommendations.

The Institution maintains its position of neutrality on issues of public policy in order to safeguard the intellectual freedom of the staff. Hence interpretations or conclusions in Brookings publications should be understood to be solely those of the authors and should not be attributed to the Institution, to its trustees, officers, or other staff members, or to the organizations that support its research.

Foreword

SLOW PROGRESS in combating hunger and malnutrition in developing countries has led governments and international organizations to join in efforts to improve agriculture and to restrict population growth. But there remain substantial differences of opinion on the scope and nature of the problem, the appropriate ways to deal with it, and the prospects of success.

Almost one-half of the 460 million people that the 1974 World Food Conference classified as undernourished live in India. As the world's largest democracy and one of the two largest developing countries, India is of central importance in the debate over food and population. In this volume Fred H. Sanderson and Shyamal Roy present a comprehensive analysis of India's agricultural prospects and policies.

The first part of their study deals with the long-term trends in food-grain production. They employ statistical analysis to separate the effects of weather and technology and to examine the contributions made by irrigation, fertilizers, and improved varieties of wheat and rice. They test some popular hypotheses about price policy and institutional impediments to food production, and identify major obstacles to increasing the rate of growth of food production. They follow this with an examination of the statistical evidence on food consumption and the extent of undernutrition.

In the second part of their study, the authors project the demand for food in India to the year 2000. They examine how the increased demand could be met from domestic production, estimate the effect of the increase on future production costs, and discuss the implications of their findings for development, trade, and aid policies.

Fred H. Sanderson and Shyamal Roy prepared this study as a senior fellow and a research associate, respectively, in the Brookings Foreign Policy Studies program.

For helpful criticisms and suggestions, the authors acknowledge their indebtedness to J. S. Sarma, former member and secretary of the National Commission on Agriculture of the Government of India, now with the International Food Policy Research Institute; to John P. Lewis of Princeton University; and to David Hopper, Alan Berg, and Shlomo Reutlinger of the World Bank. They are also grateful to A. A. Johnson of the Ford Foundation, Ralph Cummings, Jr., of the Rockefeller Foundation, Dana Dalrymple of the U.S. Agency for International Development, and B. Sen of the U.S. AID Mission to India for commenting on an early draft of this study, and to those who attended a dinner-seminar held at Brookings in September 1978 for the comments made on that occasion.

They also thank Donald Stanley for statistical assistance, and Janet E. Smith for typing and retyping the manuscript with her usual care and patience. The manuscript was edited by Ellen Alston; its factual content was verified by Ellen Smith. All those whose assistance is acknowledged contributed to improving the manuscript, but the responsibility for any remaining errors of fact or interpretation remains with the authors.

The Institution is grateful to the U.S. Agency for International Development, which financed the initial stages of this study, and to the National Science Foundation, whose grant helped toward its completion. As in all Brookings studies, the views expressed here are those of the authors alone and should not be ascribed to the sponsors or to the trustees, officers, or other staff members of the Brookings Institution.

BRUCE K. MAC LAURY
President

November 1979
Washington, D.C.

Contents

1. Overview   1
   The Food-Population Crunch *1*
   The Past Quarter Century *3*
   The Next Quarter Century *6*
   Policy Implications *9*

2. Foodgrain Production: Goals and Achievements   12
   India's Development Strategy *13*
   Did It Work? *17*

3. Input Factors Affecting Production   21
   All Cereals *21*
   Wheat *26*
   Rice *32*
   Coarse Grains *38*
   Pulses *39*

4. Economic Factors   43
   Imports and Stock Management *43*
   Government Procurement and Distribution *45*
   Adequacy of Price Incentives *48*

5. Institutional Factors   57
   Land Distribution *57*
   Farm Size and Productivity *60*
   Credit *66*
   Land Tenure *67*
   Fragmentation of Holdings *70*
   Pros and Cons of Land Redistribution *70*
   Effects of Tractorization *73*
   Research and Extension *75*

6. Food Supplies and Food Consumption   77
   How Much Undernutrition? *79*

7. India's Food Demand at a Population of One Billion   91
    Factors Affecting Demand *91*
    Projected Demand for Foodgrains *99*
    Projected Demand for Other Foods *102*
    Intercountry Comparison *103*
    Projected Food Consumption under Alternative Assumptions *104*
    Can Hunger Be Eliminated? *106*
    Interpretation of the Results *108*

8. Meeting the Food Demand from Domestic Production   110
    Land and Water Resources *110*
    Output *117*
    Implications for Production Costs *125*

9. Policy Implications   131
    Are Our Projections Realistic? *131*
    The Role of Foreign Trade *137*
    Investment Requirements *139*
    Increased Government Support for Agricultural Investment *143*
    Price Policy and Supply Management *146*
    Ensuring a Minimum Level of Nutrition *148*
    The Role of International Assistance *150*

    Appendix: Statistical Data   155

Text Tables

1-1. Daily Consumption of Calories and Protein as Derived from Principal
     Foods, India, 1975   2
1-2. Summary of Food Demand Projections, India, 1975–2000   7
1-3. Summary of Crop Output and Input Projections, India, 1975–2000   8
2-1. Public Sector Outlays on Agriculture, India, 1950–51 to 1982–83   14
2-2. Targets and Achievements of Agricultural Development under Five-Year
     Plans, India, 1950–51 to 1982–83   18
2-3. Foodgrain Production, Area, and Yield, India, 1950–51 to 1977–78   20
3-1. Yields and Factors Affecting Yields, All Cereals, India, 1960–61
     to 1977–78   24
3-2. Wheat Production, Area, and Yield, India, 1951–52 to 1977–78   26
3-3. Actual and Weather-Adjusted Yields, Fertilizer Consumption,
     and Unexplained Residuals, Wheat, India, 1957–58 to 1977–78   28
3-4. Percent of Area under HYVs, Yields of HYVs, and Percent Irrigated,
     Wheat, India, 1966–67 to 1977–78   30
3-5. Rice Production, Area, and Yield, India, 1951–52 to 1977–78   33
3-6. Actual and Weather-Adjusted Yields, Fertilizer Consumption,
     and Unexplained Residuals, Rice, India, 1957–58 to 1977–78   35
3-7. Area under HYVs and Area Irrigated, Rice, India, 1966–67 to 1977–78 36
3-8. Area, Production, and Yield of Major Coarse Grains and Pulses,
     India, 1950–51 to 1977–78   40
4-1. Foodgrain Production Shortfalls, Releases from Stocks,
     and Net Imports, India, 1960–61 to 1977–78   44

4-2. Indian Government Procurement and Distribution of Foodgrains,
1960–61 to 1977–78   47

4-3. Open-Market and Government Procurement Prices of Wheat
and Quantities Sold, India, 1966–67 to 1975–76   49

4-4. Open-Market and Government Procurement Prices of Rice
and Quantities Sold, India, 1967–68 to 1975–76   50

4-5. Cost of Production of Wheat in Three Major Wheat-Growing States,
India, 1971–72   52

4-6. Cost of Production of Rice in Five Major Rice-Growing States,
India, 1971–72   52

4-7. Cost of Production of Wheat in Punjab, 1970–71 to 1974–75   53

5-1. Farms, by Size of Operating Unit, India, 1970–71   58

5-2. Land Ownership, by Size of Holding, India, 1953–54, 1961–62,
and 1971–72   59

5-3. Farm Size and Value of Production per Net Cropped Hectare, Punjab,
1971–72   62

5-4. Value of Production, by Farm Size, All India, 1968–71   63

5-5. Cropping Intensity and Percent of Cultivated Area Irrigated,
by Farm Size, India, 1970–71   63

5-6. Fertilizer Consumption, by Farm Size, India, 1968–69 to 1970–71   64

5-7. Percent of Farmers Using HYVs, by Farm Size, India, 1968–69 to
1970–71   65

5-8. Percent of Sown Area under HYVs, by Farm Size, India, 1968–69 to
1970–71   65

5-9. Rural Credit, by Farm Size, India, 1970–71   67

5-10. Percent of Agricultural Credit Received from Various Sources
and Average Interest Rates, by Farm Size, India, 1970–71   67

5-11. Consolidation of Holdings, Selected States, India, 1973–74   71

6-1. Foodgrain Production, Net Imports, Changes in Stocks, and
Net Availability, India, 1960–61 to 1977–78   78

6-2. Annual Per Capita Consumption of Foodgrains, by Expenditure Class,
India, 1964–65   81

6-3. Calories Derived from Foodgrains, Other Foods of Vegetable Origin,
and Foods of Animal Origin, by Expenditure Class, Total Population,
India, 1975   82

6-4. Calories Derived from Foodgrains, Other Foods of Vegetable Origin,
and Foods of Animal Origin, by Expenditure Class, Rural Population,
India, 1975   83

6-5. Calories Derived from Foodgrains, Other Foods of Vegetable Origin,
and Foods of Animal Origin, by Expenditure Class, Urban Population,
India, 1975   84

6-6. Average Daily Per Capita Intake of Calories, by Expenditure Class,
Calcutta, 1969–70   86

6-7. Average Daily Calorie Intake of the Rural Population of Nine States,
by Income, India, 1970s   86

6-8. Average Daily Consumption of Calories per Capita, by Expenditure
Class, Rural Population, India, 1971–72   88

6-9. Average Daily Consumption of Calories per Capita, by Expenditure
Class, Urban Population, India, 1971–72   89

7-1. Age-Specific Fertility Rates, India, 1964–65, 1969, and 1972   93

7-2. Population of India, 1960–70, and Projections for 1975–2000   94

7-3. Per Capita Income, India, 1970 and 1975, and Projections for
1980–2000   95

7-4. Consumption of Foodgrains, Other Foods of Vegetable Origin, and Foods
of Animal Origin, India, 1975, and Projections for 1990 and 2000   97

7-5. Demand for Foodgrains for Direct Human Consumption, India, 1975,
and Projections for 1990 and 2000   99

7-6. Seed Requirements for Foodgrains, India, 1975, and Projections for
1990 and 2000   100

7-7. Total Demand for Foodgrains, India, 1975, and Projections for 1990
and 2000   101

7-8. Demand for Vegetable Foods Other than Foodgrains, India, 1975,
and Projections for 1990 and 2000   102

7-9. Demand for Foods of Animal Origin, India, 1975, and Projections
for 1990 and 2000   103

7-10. Food Consumption in India Compared with That in Other Countries,
1975, and Projections for India, 1990 and 2000   104

7-11. Effects of Alternative Assumptions on Projected Food Consumption,
India, 1990 and 2000   105

8-1. Land Utilization, India, Selected Years, 1950–51 to 1975–76   111

8-2. Net Irrigated Area, by Source, India, Selected Years, 1950–51
to 1975–76   114

8-3. Cropping Intensity Indexes, India, Selected Years, 1950–51 to 1975–76 115

8-4. Net and Gross Sown and Irrigated Areas, India, 1975, and Projections
for 1990 and 2000   116

8-5. Gross Sown and Irrigated Areas, All Foodgrains, India, 1975,
and Projections for 1990 and 2000   117

8-6. Gross Sown and Irrigated Areas, by Foodgrain, India, 1975,
and Projections for 1990 and 2000   118

8-7. Average Yields of Foodgrains on Irrigated and Unirrigated Land,
India, 1975, and Projections for 1990 and 2000   119

8-8. Factors Affecting Yields of Irrigated Foodgrains, India, 1975,
and Projections for 1990 and 2000   120

8-9. Fertilizer Dosages for Unirrigated Foodgrains, India, 1975,
and Projections for 1990 and 2000   121

8-10. Total Output of Foodgrains and Input Requirements, India, 1975,
and Projections for 1990 and 2000   121

8-11. Area, Production, and Yields of Other Food Crops, India, 1975   122

8-12. Yields of Other Food Crops, India, 1975, and Projections for 1990
and 2000   123

8-13. Irrigated Area and Fertilizer Consumption, Other Food Crops, India,
1975, and Projections for 1990 and 2000   124

8-14. Area under Other Food Crops, India, 1975, and Projections for 1990
and 2000   124

8-15. Total Output of Other Food Crops and Input Requirements, India,
1975, and Projections for 1990 and 2000   124

8-16. Summary of Input Requirements for Industrial and Other Nonfood
Crops, India, 1975, and Projections for 1990 and 2000   125

8-17. Estimated Costs of Irrigation, India, 1975–2000   128

9-1. Annual Growth Rates, India, 1950–75, and Projections for 1975–2000   132

9-2. Authors' Projections Compared with Projections by the National
Commission on Agriculture, India, 1975–2000   134

9-3. Projected Annual Growth Rates, India, Various Studies and Years   136

9-4. Net Food Import Projections, India, Various Studies, 1985 or 1990   137

9-5. India's Exports and Imports, Annual Average, 1973–74 to 1975–76   138

9-6. Estimated Capital Costs of Irrigation, India, 1975–2000   140

9-7. Remaining Groundwater Potential and Factors Affecting Exploitation,
by State, India   141

9-8. World Bank Loans and International Development Association Credits
for Indian Agriculture, Commitments, Fiscal Years 1973–79   151

Appendix Tables

A-1. Rainfall Indexes, Various Crops, India, 1951–52 to 1977–78   156

A-2. Yields and Factors Affecting Yields, All Cereals, India, 1951–52
to 1977–78   157

A-3. Gross Cropped Area, Net Cropped Area, and Cropping Intensity, India,
1950–51 to 1975–76   158

A-4. Expenditure per Capita on Roots, Vegetables, Fruits, Nuts, Sugar,
and Edible Oils, by Expenditure Class, India, 1964–65   159

A-5. Expenditure per Capita on Dairy Products, Meat, Eggs, and Fish,
by Expenditure Class, India, 1964–65   160

A-6. Population, by Expenditure Class, India, 1964–65   161

Figures

1-1. Indexes of Foodgrain Production, Population, and Per Capita
Production, India, 1950–51 to 1977–78   4

2-1. Foodgrain Production, Gross Area, and Yield, India, 1950–51
to 1977–78   19

3-1. Actual and Weather-Adjusted Yields, All Cereals, India, 1960–61
to 1977–78   23

3-2. Weather-Adjusted Yields, Fertilizer Consumption, and Unexplained
Residuals, Wheat, India, 1957–58 to 1977–78   29

3-3. Weather-Adjusted Yields, Fertilizer Consumption, and Unexplained
Residuals, Rice, India, 1957–58 to 1977–78   34

4-1. Indexes of Profitability, Fertilizer Consumption, and Weather-Adjusted
Yields, Wheat, India, 1961–62 to 1977–78   54

4-2. Indexes of Profitability, Fertilizer Consumption, and Weather-Adjusted
Yields, Rice, India, 1961–62 to 1977–78   55

7-1. Rural Food Consumption and Income, India, 1975, and Projections
for 1990 and 2000   98

7-2. Urban Food Consumption and Income, India, 1975, and Projections
for 1990 and 2000   98

A-1. Rainfall Indexes and Yield, Various Crops, India, 1951–52 to 1977–78   162

CHAPTER ONE

Overview

IT IS NOT SURPRISING that the food situation in India is a perennial subject of international concern. India's population of 650 million accounts for one-seventh of the world's population and one-third of the population of the third world. Its average per capita food consumption is barely sufficient to meet the minimum daily requirement of 2,100 calories.[1] About one-third of the Indian population is too poor to afford even this minimum diet necessary to sustain a moderate level of activity. These more than 200 million Indians represent about half of the world's chronically undernourished people.[2] Their situation becomes critical whenever the monsoon fails to deliver enough rain to produce an average crop. In such years, average food consumption may drop by as much as 10 percent, despite massive grain imports.[3] International food aid, government stockpiling, and government food procurement and distribution through "fair price shops" and food-for-work programs have helped to prevent outright starvation. But inevitably, the poor bear the brunt of recurrent crop failures.

The Food-Population Crunch

There is all the more reason for concern because this situation has not improved significantly during the past quarter century. True, the production of foodgrains (which, as shown in table 1-1, account for three-

1. See table 1-1 and chapter 6.
2. Estimated at 462 million in 1970. United Nations World Food Conference, *Assessment of the World Food Situation: Present and Future*, Item 8 of the Provisional Agenda, E/CONF. 65/3 (Rome: November 5–16, 1974), p. 66.
3. See table 6-1.

Table 1-1. *Daily Consumption of Calories and Protein as Derived from Principal Foods, India, 1975*

Foodstuff	Number of calories	Grams of protein
Total vegetable foods	**1,943**	**44.8**
Total foodgrains	1,507	40.5
Cereals	1,371	32.4
Rice	665	12.5
Wheat	344	10.0
Coarse grains	362	9.9
Pulses	136	8.1
Other vegetable foods	436	4.3
Starchy roots and tubers	36	0.5
Sugar and sugar products	199	0.5
Nuts, oilseeds, and vegetable oils	130	0.7
Vegetables, fruits, and miscellaneous (spices, stimulants)	71	2.6
Total animal foods	**102**[a]	**5.7**
Meat	7	0.6
Eggs	0	0.0
Fish	5	1.0
Dairy products	88	4.1
All food	**2,045**	**50.5**

Source: Unpublished data supplied by the Food and Agriculture Organization of the United Nations.
a. Includes 2 calories from animal fats other than butter.

fourths of the calories and four-fifths of the protein in the Indian diet) has been rising at an annual rate of 2.8 percent, which ranks with the growth rates achieved in the developed world.[4] This, in itself, is a significant accomplishment. But population increased almost as fast, at an annual rate of 2.2 percent. As a result, the average yearly increase in per capita production has been only 0.6 percent.[5]

While the upward trend of foodgrain production has been fairly steady over the period as a whole, it is possible to distinguish between periods of more rapid growth and periods of stagnation. These fluctuations have given rise to successive waves of optimism and pessimism concerning India's food production performance and future prospects. Despair gave way to euphoria as the country worked its way out of the drought of the

4. The official Indian usage is followed here, in which "foodgrains" is defined to include all grains and pulses. "Grains" or "cereals" are defined to include rice, wheat, and coarse grains but not pulses. All growth rates given are average compound rates, unless otherwise stated. Crop years are July to June.
5. See figure 1-1. Trends are exponential.

mid-sixties, achieving a 50 percent production gain in five years. The temptation was great to attribute all of this gain to the "green revolution"; the introduction of high-yielding varieties seemed to have solved India's food problem.

Renewed pessimism set in when India failed to make further gains in the following four years. Some observers concluded that the green revolution was a myth. Others blamed government policies for not offering sufficient incentives to agriculture,[6] or India's institutional structure for denying adequate help to its small farmers.[7] Still others pointed to shortages of energy and fertilizer.[8] Anxiety was sharpened by the fact that the resumption of large food imports by India coincided with a series of major crop shortfalls in the USSR and North America, which depleted grain stocks and caused world grain prices to triple.[9]

Large crops since 1975, which have led to a record buildup of grain stocks in India and a sharp drop in imports, have now set the stage for another wave of self-congratulations, which risks leading to a relaxation of efforts to solve the food problem. Clearly, a better understanding is needed of the reasons for the trends and variations in grain production and their implications for India's future.

The Past Quarter Century

The strongest overall impression of foodgrain production in India in the last twenty-five years is the sustained upward trend—matched, to be sure, by an almost equally rapid rise in population (figure 1-1). In that period, foodgrain production has doubled, and population has risen by 70 percent.

A large part of the fluctuations of output around the trend can be explained by weather conditions (see figures 3-1, 3-2, 3-3). But closer analysis of the factors subject to human control reveals that the sources of

6. Theodore W. Schultz, "Farm Entrepreneurs, Incentives, and Economic Policy," paper presented at Workshop on Resources, Incentives and Agriculture, University of Chicago, September 26–28, 1977.

7. Keith Griffin, *The Political Economy of Agrarian Change: An Essay on the Green Revolution* (Harvard University Press, 1974).

8. Roger Revelle, "Energy Use in Rural India," *Science*, vol. 192 (June 4, 1976), pp. 969–75.

9. Fred H. Sanderson, "The Great Food Fumble," *Science*, vol. 188 (May 9, 1975), pp. 502–09.

Figure 1-1. *Indexes of Foodgrain Production, Population, and Per Capita Production, India, 1950–51 to 1977–78*

Index: 1950–51 to 1952–53 = 100

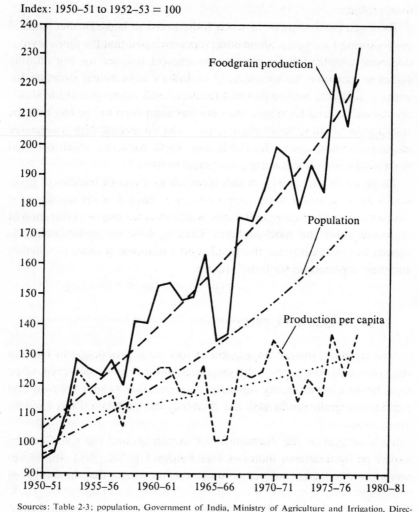

Sources: Table 2-3; population, Government of India, Ministry of Agriculture and Irrigation, Directorate of Economics and Statistics, *Bulletin on Food Statistics, 1978*, 28th issue (Delhi: Controller of Publications, 1979), table 11, p. 124. Trends are exponential.

progress have been more varied than one might suppose. In the 1950s, almost half of the output growth was accomplished by increasing the area under foodgrains and the rate of double cropping. Since 1960, the gross area planted has increased by only 10 percent; most of the 50 percent growth in output was accomplished by increasing yields per gross hectare (see table 2-3).

The analysis of yields reveals two periods of rapid growth that cannot be explained by weather factors: 1966–67 to 1970–71 and 1973–74 to 1977–78 (figure 3-1). The first of these surges can be traced to the successful introduction of high-yielding varieties. This "green revolution" was largely confined to wheat grown on irrigated land in the northwestern part of the country (see chapter 3). The second surge is too recent to permit a complete analysis, but it can be traced largely to a significant increase in the (weather-adjusted) yields of rice—a crop which heretofore had shown a rather sluggish response to the new technology. In all instances, however, progress was crucially dependent upon the continuing expansion of irrigation facilities and the steady increase (interrupted only briefly in 1973 and 1974) in the availability and use of fertilizer (see table 3-1).

Economic factors may have played a role in stimulating foodgrain production in certain periods and in holding it back at other times. In general, however, farmers' returns seem to have been adequate to achieve otherwise attainable increases in inputs. Technological factors, then, rather than lack of profitability, were the overriding limiting factors (see chapter 4).

There is a widespread impression that increased foodgrain production in India is hampered by institutions and policies that favor the large owner-operated farm at the expense of the labor-intensive small farm, which can achieve higher yields per hectare. This study examines some of the specific issues bearing on this question—such as land distribution, land tenure, the fragmentation of holdings, tractorization, and the availability of credit—and their effects on food production and distribution. The available evidence indicates that small farms are indeed more productive per unit of land than larger farms, but that the green revolution has narrowed the gap. There are indications that the smallest farmers have greater difficulty in obtaining low-cost credit from credit institutions than do owners of medium and large farms; this problem may have impeded the small farmer's use of fertilizers and other purchased inputs. The green revolution has reinforced the trend toward operation by owners of land previously cultivated by tenants and sharecroppers, but there is no conclusive evidence that this has had adverse effects on production per unit of land. Contrary to what might be expected, the introduction of tractors led to *more* intensive cultivation in the special circumstances of Punjab and Haryana, the areas where tractors are now used on a significant scale. Land redistribution has proceeded at a slow pace: the 1.6 million hectares declared surplus under the Indian land reform laws will provide land for only 800,000 two-hectare farms. A more radical land redistribution would have both favorable and unfavorable effects on food production and probable adverse effects on the marketable surplus required to feed the rapidly growing urban centers (see chapter 5).

The record harvests since 1975 are encouraging, but they do not mean that India is over the hump. Now that production is back on trend, it is clear that the problem, while not worsening, continues much the same as it has always been: a trend of food production that is rising a step ahead of population growth, but not fast enough to allow a satisfactory improvement in per capita food consumption levels.

The Next Quarter Century

The demand and supply projections put forward in this study represent expectations that we consider realistic in the light of our analysis of past trends. A basic assumption underlying the projections is that the demand for food in India will continue to be determined in a market which is essentially free. Foods other than foodgrains are included in the projections because their importance in the Indian diet is likely to grow in the years to come.

The principal factors determining the future demand for food are population, income, and the degree of urbanization. We project population to approach the 1 billion mark by the year 2000. A main feature of our projections is a gradual acceleration in the rate of economic growth as reflected in per capita incomes and the degree of urbanization. We project average incomes to increase by 140 percent between 1975 and the end of the century; we also project the proportion of the urban population to approximately double, from 22 percent in 1975 to 41 percent in 2000.

On these assumptions, we expect the demand for foodgrains to double and the total demand for food to rise from 146 million metric tons (grain equivalent) in 1975 to 333 million tons in 2000. A lower rate of economic growth, however (say, half the rate projected above), would result in a lower demand for food (less than a doubling). The demand projections are summarized in table 1-2.

This study goes on to show how the projected demand could be met

Table 1-2. *Summary of Food Demand Projections, India, 1975–2000*

Item	1975	2000	Annual change (percent)
Population (millions)	611	993	2.0
Urban population (percent of total)	22	41	...
High economic growth alternative[a]			
Income per capita (1975 = 100)	100	239	3.5
Per capita demand for foodgrains[b] (kilograms)	188	222	0.7[c]
Per capita demand for food (kilograms, grain equivalent)	239	335	1.4[d]
Total demand for foodgrains[b] (millions of metric tons)	115	220	2.7
Total demand for food (millions of metric tons, grain equivalent)	146	333	3.4
Low economic growth alternative[e]			
Total demand for foodgrains[b] (million of metric tons)	115	202	2.3
Total demand for food (millions of metric tons, grain equivalent)	146	269	2.5

Source: Authors' projections, from tables 7-2, 7-3, and 7-11.
a. Table 7-11, alternative A.
b. All uses.
c. Implied income elasticity, 0.2.
d. Implied income elasticity, 0.4.
e. Table 7-11, alternative C + D.

from domestic production. The past annual growth rate of foodgrain production (2.8 percent) would be sufficient to meet our projected demand for foodgrains (including grain for livestock feeding). Allowance must be made, however, for the anticipated rapid increase in the demand for other food crops (oilseeds, sugar, and vegetables and fruits). To meet this demand, total food crop production will have to be speeded up to an annual rate of 3.4 percent, under our high income assumption; under our low income assumption, an average annual growth rate of 2.5 percent would be sufficient (see table 1-2).

What would it take to increase food production by 128 percent in twenty-five years? Various combinations of extensive and intensive development are possible; but judging from past trends and existing potential, it could probably be accomplished most efficiently in the manner outlined in table 1-3. Since there is little idle land suitable for cultivation, we project no increase in net sown area. We expect, however, that gross sown area (including land needed for nonfood crops) can be expanded by

Table 1-3. *Summary of Crop Output and Input Projections, India,
1975–2000*

Item	1975	2000	2000 as percent of 1975	Annual change (percent)
All crops				
Net sown area (millions of hectares)	142	144	101	0.0
Gross sown area (millions of hectares)	171	203	119	0.7
Cropping intensity (percent)	120	141	118	0.6
Net irrigated area (millions of hectares)	34	57	168	2.1
Gross irrigated area (millions of hectares)	43	94	219	3.1
Cropping intensity (percent)	124	165	133	1.1
Fertilizer consumption, total (millions of metric tons, NPK)[a]	3.0	17.8	593	7.4
Fertilizer consumption, per gross sown hectare (kilograms per hectare)	17.5	87.7	501	6.6
Foodgrains				
Production (millions of metric tons)	121	220	182	2.4
Yields, total (kilograms per gross sown hectare)	943	1,889	200	2.8
Yields, irrigated land (kilograms per hectare)	1,525	2,525	166	2.0
All food crops				
Production (millions of metric tons, grain equivalent)	146	333	228	3.4

Source: Authors' projections, from tables 7-11, 8-4, 8-7, 8-10, 8-13, 8-15. Figures are rounded.
a. Expressed in pure nutrients of NPK (nitrogen, phosphorus, potassium).

20 percent (32 million hectares) by double cropping. The remainder of the required increase in production would be brought about by raising yields. We project yields of foodgrains to double in the next twenty-five years (as compared with a 60 percent increase in the past twenty-five years). Yields on irrigated land are projected to increase by 65 percent.

The projected increase in cropping intensity and yield per crop will require doubling the water now supplied by irrigation, as well as a sixfold increase in fertilizer use. The net irrigated area is projected to increase by 68 percent (23 million hectares) by the year 2000. With rising cropping intensities on the irrigated land, the gross irrigated area is projected to more than double, from 43 million hectares in 1975 to 94 million hectares by the end of the century. Fertilizer consumption is projected to rise from 3 million tons in 1975 to 18 million tons.

Are these growth rates realistic? The projected growth in net irrigated area is roughly in line with the trend, but the absolute increase (23 million hectares) is considerably greater than the 13 million hectares brought under irrigation in the past twenty-five years. The projected doubling of the *gross* irrigated area is, perhaps, a better measure of the effort required. Water will have to be conserved through greater efficiency in water use, and it will have to be stored, above or below ground, for use in the dry season if the projected increase in the cropping ratio is to be achieved. Failing this, an even greater effort would have to be made to increase yields.

The projected rate of growth of fertilizer use is also in line with past trends. Fertilizer consumption, which tripled between 1967 and 1977, is projected to almost triple again in the next fifteen years and to approximately double in the last decade of the century.

The projected levels of food production are modest in relation to India's production potential. Even in the year 2000, the projections would leave India with a substantially underutilized agricultural plant. The projected cropping intensity of 141 would still be less than past or current levels in China, Taiwan, Korea, Bangladesh, and Japan. Fertilizer use, at 88 kilograms per gross cropped hectare, would be only about one-fourth current levels in northwestern Europe and Japan. Average grain yields, at 1.9 tons per hectare, would be about one-half of those already achieved in Japan, Korea, Taiwan, northwestern Europe, and the United States. The projections for irrigation would still leave a modest margin for further expansion of the irrigated area and a significant margin for further improvements in the efficiency of water use.

Policy Implications

Massive investments in irrigation, fertilizer, and energy will be required to achieve the projected growth in food output. The cost of the additional irrigation alone (including replacement costs of tubewells) will be on the order of $75 billion, or $3 billion per year (in 1975 dollars). About $14 billion ($550 million annually) will be required to install the additional fertilizer production capacity. Total agricultural investment requirements may thus be estimated at about $115 billion, or $4.5 billion per year (see chapter 9). Our analysis suggests, however, that these investments are likely to pay off without any increase in food prices, in real terms (see chapter 8).

With a sustained effort of this magnitude, India has the capacity of producing enough food to meet the prospective demand. The fact that food self-sufficiency is attainable does not mean that it should be the overriding goal of Indian policy to eliminate all food imports. India may well find its advantage in continuing to import some of its requirements for staple foods that can be procured cheaply in the world market, while paying for these imports with the proceeds of labor-intensive agricultural and manufactured products which it can produce more efficiently than other countries. The extent to which India can rely on international trade to meet some of its food requirements will depend on the international competitiveness of its exports (which will, in turn, depend on its domestic economic policies) and on the willingness of others, particularly the industrial countries, to keep their doors open to exports by developing countries.

In any event, food imports can make only a marginal contribution to India's food supply; the country will undoubtedly continue to rely on domestic production for the great bulk (at present over 95 percent) of its food requirements. Meeting the projected increase in the demand for food will require an accelerated agricultural development effort, particularly in the next fifteen years. The need for increased emphasis on food production has been recognized in India's current development plan and in the programs of the World Bank. Agricultural investments envisaged in the new (sixth) plan ($5 billion annually) seem to be in line with our projections.

But accelerated growth will not come cheaply or easily. While the major investment needs are in irrigation, fertilizers, and electrification, these programs must go hand-in-hand with improved drainage, crop protection, storage, and distribution. An intensified research effort is needed to maintain the momentum of genetic improvements necessary to take advantage of more adequate and regular water and fertilizer supplies. Equally urgent is the improvement of agricultural education and extension services, and of agricultural credit facilities, to enable small farmers, in particular, to take advantage of the new technology. Small farmers should also benefit from greater government support of cooperative arrangements for the purchase of inputs, the installation of tubewells, and the storage and marketing of farm produce.

International assistance will continue to be required to support India's agricultural development effort. To the extent that aid is supplied in the form of food to meet import requirements, care should be taken to ensure that such assistance does not serve as an excuse for neglecting domestic agricultural production. Consideration should be given to earmarking sales proceeds from food aid for job-creating development projects, particularly in agriculture or related activities.

President Carter, in his statement before the Indian Parliament,[10] said he was impressed with the creative direction the government of India has taken in its strengthened commitment to rural improvement; he was equally impressed with its industrial achievements. Indeed, there is reason for optimism. India is not the hopeless case it is sometimes made out to be. It is a poor and crowded country endowed with vast resources for agricultural and industrial development. Substantial progress is already being made in developing these resources, but excessive population growth has stood in the way of economic growth and improved living standards. Now there are indications that population growth is slowing down and income growth accelerating. There is increased recognition of the important role agriculture must play in the process of modernization and industrialization of the Indian economy. There is every reason to believe that by the end of this century Indian agriculture, given the means, can meet the demand for food of a population of 1 billion, whose incomes will be well over twice what they are today.

10. "Remarks before the Indian Parliament, January 2, 1978," *Weekly Compilation of Presidential Documents,* vol. 14 (1978), pp. 5–11.

CHAPTER TWO

Foodgrain Production: Goals and Achievements

IT IS WIDELY BELIEVED that Indian agriculture has been held back because successive Indian governments have given it a low priority. Progress could have been much faster, so the argument goes, if Indian planners, particularly in the fifties and early sixties, had not been bent on the rapid development of a modern industrial sector, with excessive emphasis on large-scale, capital-intensive industries such as steel, heavy engineering, chemicals, and so forth. That development strategy (often associated with P. C. Mahalanobis, mastermind of the second five-year plan), failed to mobilize the only resource that is in ample supply in a developing country, namely, labor. The result was rising unemployment (or underemployment), the flight of population from the countryside to the cities, an increasingly skewed distribution of incomes, and a slower overall rate of income growth than could have been achieved by a strategy focused on the development of agriculture and cottage industries.[1] The rural development strategy, which is now as widely accepted by development economists as the strategy of rapid industrialization was in the 1950s, has led to a shift in emphasis in development policies.

It may appear, in retrospect, that greater emphasis should have been placed on agriculture and labor-intensive industries. But the issue is not as clear-cut as the revisionist school would have us believe. A strong case could be made for the early efforts to develop an industrial base, not only in political terms,[2] but also from the point of view of long-term economic development. Expenditures on transportation, electric power, and basic

1. For a discussion of the issue, see John W. Mellor, *The New Economics of Growth: A Strategy for India and the Developing World* (Cornell University Press, 1976).

2. Mellor points out, for example, that the strategy of rapid industrialization gave the country a unifying theme and served the aspirations of the governing elite for transforming India into a modern world power (ibid., pp. 2–6).

industries are not frivolous expenditures comparable to the building of the pyramids. Investments in capital-intensive industries can be justified where foreign-exchange constraints are expected to prevent a flow of essential capital-goods imports adequate to sustain the desired rate of economic development.[3] It is certainly arguable that these investments are now beginning to pay off in a stronger balance-of-payments position and a higher future rate of economic growth than would have resulted from a strategy giving overriding priority to maximizing employment and the satisfaction of basic human needs. Socialist and market economies alike face this difficult choice between short-term and long-term returns.

India's Development Strategy

Closer analysis of successive Indian development plans indicates, moreover, that the allocation of investment funds controlled by the central government was not as unbalanced, and the changes in emphasis less radical, than might appear from the sound and fury of subsequent debate. As table 2-1 shows, the share allocated to agriculture and rural development, which represented about one-third of planned outlays in the First Plan,[4] never dropped much below one-fourth.[5] In absolute amounts, it increased over fourteenfold from the First to the Fifth Plan. To these figures must be added at least another 50 percent in private investments in land improvement, tubewells and other minor irrigation projects, buildings, tools, and equipment.[6]

3. See John P. Lewis, *Quiet Crisis in India: Economic Development and American Policy* (Brookings Institution, 1962), for a spirited defense of what was then regarded as a "balanced development" strategy.

4. The relatively larger share of agriculture in the First Plan was apparently due to the lack of industrial projects that were ready to be implemented. See ibid., pp. 45–46.

5. It is also worth noting that the agricultural outlays shown in table 2-1 do not include rural development expenditures such as rural roads, water supply for households, health and family welfare, education, nutrition, social welfare, housing, traditional cottage and household industries, and outlays for electric power development indirectly attributable to rural areas. If these items are included, the percentage of total plan outlays directed toward agricultural and rural development rises to 37.5 percent in the Fifth Plan and 43.1 percent in the Sixth Plan. See Government of India, Planning Commission, *Draft Five Year Plan, 1978–83* (Delhi: Controller of Publications, 1978), p. 18.

6. Private investments in agriculture and irrigation are estimated at 6.25 billion rupees during the Second Plan, 8.0 billion during the Third Plan, and 16.0 billion during the Fourth Plan. *Report of the National Commission on Agriculture, 1976*, pt. 2: *Policy and Strategy*, Government of India, Ministry of Agriculture and Irrigation (Delhi: Controller of Publications, 1976), p. 16.

Table 2-1. *Public Sector Outlays*[a] *on Agriculture,*[b] *India, 1950–51 to 1982–83*
Amounts in billions of rupees

Type of outlay	First Plan, 1950–51 to 1955–56 Amount	Percent of total	Second Plan, 1956–57 to 1960–61 Amount	Percent of total	Third Plan, 1961–62 to 1965–66 Amount	Percent of total	Fourth Plan, 1969–70 to 1973–74 Amount	Percent of total	Fifth Plan, 1974–75 to 1977–78[c] Amount	Percent of total	Sixth Plan, 1978–79 to 1982–83 Amount	Percent of total
Agriculture[d]	2.17	10.8	2.76	6.0	7.25	8.4	19.66	12.4	45.91	11.7	97.00	14.0
Major irrigation[e]	4.32[f]	21.5	4.20	9.1	6.65	7.7	13.54	8.6	34.34	8.7	79.25	11.4
Fertilizer and pesticides	0.09	0.4	0.37	0.8	2.25	2.6	4.93	3.1	15.55	3.9	16.88	2.4
Rural electrification[g]	0.08	0.4	0.75	1.6	1.53	1.8	7.23	4.6	8.00[h]	2.0	14.50	2.1
Community development[i]	0.82	4.1	2.53	5.5	3.64	4.2	3.55	2.2	5.03	1.3	6.25	0.9
Total agricultural outlays	7.48	37.2	10.61	23.1	21.32	24.9	48.91	31.0	108.83	27.7	213.88	30.8
Total plan outlays	20.13	100.0	46.00	100.0	85.76	100.0	157.79	100.0	393.22	100.0	693.80	100.0

Sources: Government of India, Planning Commission, *Selected Plan Statistics* (New Delhi, 1959); GOI, Planning Commission, *Review of the First Five Year Plan* (Delhi: Manager of Publications, 1957); GOI, Planning Commission, *Second Five Year Plan*, 6 vols. (Delhi: Government of India Press, 1957); GOI, Planning Commission, *Third Five Year Plan* (Delhi: Manager of Publications, 1961); GOI, Planning Commission, *The Fourth Plan: Mid-Term Appraisal* (New Delhi, 1971); GOI, Ministry of Agriculture and Irrigation, Directorate of Economics and Statistics, *Indian Agriculture in Brief*, 13th ed. (Delhi: Controller of Publications, 1974), and 16th ed. (Delhi: Controller of Publications, 1978) [hereafter, *Indian Agriculture in Brief*]; GOI, Planning Commission, *Draft Five Year Plan, 1978–83* (Delhi: Controller of Publications, 1978).

a. First through Fifth Plans, expenditures; Sixth Plan, planned outlays.
b. See footnote 5 to this chapter.
c. The Fifth Plan was terminated one year early; figures are for four years.
d. Includes minor irrigation.
e. Includes flood control.
f. Includes power.
g. Excludes institutional finance.
h. Estimated.
i. Includes cooperation.

Roughly one-third of total central government outlays went to economic infrastructure projects (power, transportation, and communications), which benefit the economy as a whole, including agriculture. The proportion of funds directed toward industry proper (excluding fertilizer plants), although rising, did not exceed one-fourth of the total.

Whether this was the right balance depends, of course, on what weight should properly be attached to different objectives of economic development. Both in India and elsewhere the emphasis has shifted gradually from preoccupation with industrial growth toward greater concern for immediate improvements in employment opportunities and incomes of low-income groups, particularly in the rural areas. From that perspective it would have been better to devote a larger proportion of central government funds to agriculture and related sectors.

But progress does not depend only on the funds allocated to agriculture; it also depends on how effectively they are used. It was reasonable to expect that with the completion of some major irrigation projects and the expansion of the cultivated area in the 1950s, substantial advances in agricultural productivity per hectare could be achieved at a lower cost in public investment. In fact, successive plans reflect a progressive shift from major to minor irrigation and increased emphasis on fertilizer production—projects that could be expected to yield a high return per rupee invested. Of equal importance was the development in the 1960s of new short-stemmed varieties of wheat and rice that could take advantage of improved and more regular supplies of water and fertilizer.

A further indispensable step was to tie the new technology together in a "package," involving assured water, fertilizer, high-yielding seed varieties, and improved cultivating practices, which could be disseminated in areas where conditions were favorable. The package approach was adopted in the Third Plan, following a report in 1959 by a team of American experts sponsored by the Ford Foundation.[7] The Intensive Agricultural District Program, as it was called, was introduced in seven districts and later extended to sixteen districts, covering about 300 community development blocks. A further expansion, to 1,200 blocks, took place under the Intensive Agricultural Area Program during the Fourth Plan. In fact, the Fourth Plan strategy of agricultural development was based on

7. Ford Foundation, Agricultural Production Team, *Report on India's Food Crisis and Steps to Meet It* (Delhi: Government of India, Ministry of Food and Agriculture and Ministry of Community Development and Cooperation, 1959).

the exploitation of the high-yielding varieties and multiple cropping program.[8]

It is often argued that Indian agriculture has been held back by a price policy that provided insufficient economic incentives to producers. Low Indian rice prices compared with world market levels, unfavorable product-fertilizer price ratios, unfavorable developments in real prices, and the Indian system of partial rationing and price controls—all have been cited as evidence to support this thesis. But here again, the evidence is less than conclusive. Rice prices in India are lower than world prices because production costs are lower than in the United States, the dominant supplier to the world market. In 1971–72, average prices received by Indian farmers were found to be adequate to cover production costs. Parity ratios (grain-fertilizer or grain-wholesale prices) have fluctuated over time, providing greater incentives in some periods than in others. But profitability also depends on productivity. Real gross returns per hectare, reflecting increased productivity, have shown a rising trend for both wheat and rice (see chapter 4).

The government procurement and rationing system, designed to ensure a minimum level of subsistence to the urban poor at prices they can afford, seems to have had less of an adverse effect on average farm prices than is commonly believed. In normal years, procurement prices have been 15–30 percent lower than prices in the open market. In years of bumper crops, the difference has tended to disappear altogether, though substantial price differentials tend to develop in years of shortage. But in a dual price system, prices in the open market may be expected to be above those that would prevail in a completely free market, thus offsetting, at least in part, the lower prices received in the controlled market. From the available evidence it is not possible to tell whether the weighted average prices received by producers were significantly lower than the prices that would have prevailed in a completely free market (see chapter 4).

It would have been possible, of course, to use the procurement system to support producer prices above market levels. The probable effects of such a policy are, again, less clear than might appear at first sight. Higher

8. See J. S. Sarma, "Agricultural Policy in India," address delivered at the 33rd All-India Agricultural Economics Conference (Bombay: Examiner Press for Indian Society of Agricultural Economics, 1973). Other useful analyses of Indian agricultural policies can be found in Mellor, *The New Economics of Growth;* John W. Mellor and others, *Developing Rural India: Plan and Practice* (Cornell University Press, 1968); and *Report of the National Commission on Agriculture, 1976,* pt. 2. For a perceptive analysis of organizational problems, especially at the local level, see Lewis, *Quiet Crisis in India,* chap. 6.

support prices would have stimulated food production, but the incentive effects would have been limited by the existing technological constraints (water, power, fertilizer availabilities). Food consumption would have increased in the countryside but would probably have fallen in the cities, with the urban poor feeling the most serious impact. To cushion the impact, the government would have been forced to introduce consumer subsidies, thus diverting scarce budgetary resources from economic development. On the whole, the existing system of procurement and rationing would seem to have struck a reasonable balance between producer and consumer interests and between economic and social considerations. Scrapping the system would have skewed consumption to the benefit of producers and affluent consumers, with uncertain (and probably negligible) effects on food production.

Social considerations also entered increasingly into other aspects of India's farm policy. Beginning with the Fifth Plan, India's policymakers began to lay greater stress on helping the producers who had been neglected in the initial push for increased grain production—the small farmer, the farmer in dry areas, and the landless laborer. More funds were made available to develop supplementary sources of income, such as animal husbandry and cottage industries, as well as opportunities for off-farm employment (including employment on rural infrastructure projects). Besides serving the ends of greater social justice, these programs also made a useful contribution to increasing economic productivity.

Did It Work?

How successful was India's agricultural policy in achieving its main objectives? As can be seen from table 2-2, foodgrain production[9] has tended to fall short of the targets (except in the Fifth Plan, which set a lower target for 1978–79 than the preceding plan had set for 1973–74). Inputs such as irrigation and fertilizers also failed to reached the targets set in successive plans.

The overall performance was, nevertheless, quite good. The trend of foodgrain production rose 115 percent between 1950 and 1978. The average annual rate of growth (2.8 percent) was about equal to the average rates achieved in other developing countries, as well as in the de-

9. In assessing performance, we have substituted trend production for actual production of foodgrains to eliminate the effects of weather fluctuations and other transient factors (see figure 2-1). Trends are exponential.

Table 2-2. Targets and Achievements of Agricultural Development under Five-Year Plans, India, 1950–51 to 1982–83

Item	First Plan, 1950–51 to 1955–56	Second Plan, 1956–57 to 1960–61	Third Plan, 1961–62 to 1965–66	Fourth Plan, 1969–70 to 1973–74	Fifth Plan, 1974–75 to 1977–78[a]	Sixth Plan, 1978–79 to 1982–83
Foodgrain production (millions of metric tons)						
Base year (trend)[b]	57.2	65.6	75.1	96.1	107.1	119.5
Target	62.6	81.8	101.6	129.0	125.0	140.5–144.5
Achievement						
Actual	66.9	82.0	72.3	104.7	125.6	n.a.
Trend[b]	65.6	75.1	86.1	107.1	119.5	n.a.
Additional irrigation (millions of gross hectares)						
Total						
Target	6.85	8.54	9.66	11.97	10.80	17.00
Achievement	5.13	5.74	7.31	9.78	8.10	n.a.
Major and medium						
Target	3.50	4.90	4.50	4.77	5.80	8.00
Achievement	1.30	2.10	2.10	2.55	4.30	n.a.
Minor						
Target	3.35	3.64	5.16	7.20	5.00	9.00
Achievement	3.83	3.64	5.21	7.23	3.80	n.a.
Fertilizer consumption (millions of metric tons of NPK)[c]						
Target	n.a.	0.66[d]	1.43[d]	5.50	4.80	7.85
Achievement	0.14	0.28[d]	0.71[d]	2.84	4.19	n.a.
Nitrogen consumption (millions of metric tons)						
Target	0.12	0.51	1.02	3.20	3.40	5.25
Achievement	0.11	0.21	0.58	1.83	2.89	n.a.

Sources: First through Fourth Plan figures and Fifth Plan targets, *Indian Agriculture in Brief*, pp. 204–05, 211–13; Fifth Plan achievements and Sixth Plan targets, Government of India, Planning Commission, *Draft Five Year Plan, 1978–83*, pp. 25, 129–30, 135, 137.

n.a. Not available.

a. Fifth Plan targets are for 1978–79; achievements for the four years (1974–75 to 1977–78) the Fifth Plan was in effect.

b. Trend production substituted for actual foodgrain production to eliminate the effects of weather fluctuations and other temporary factors. Trends are exponential.

c. NPK is total fertilizer consumption, by weight of principal nutrients (nitrogen, phosphorus, potassium).

d. Does not include potassium.

Figure 2-1. *Foodgrain Production, Gross Area, and Yield, India, 1950–51 to 1977–78*

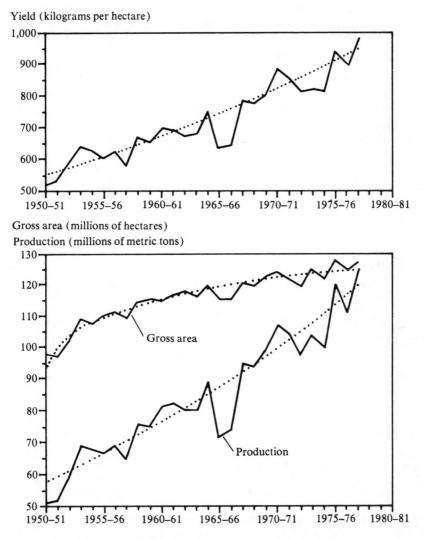

Source: Table 2-3. Trends are exponential.

veloped world. Two-thirds of the growth (1.9 percent) was due to the growth in yields, one-third (0.9 percent) to the growth in gross area sown. The contribution of yield growth has risen over time, while the contribution of area expansion has declined (see figure 2-1). About 40

Food Trends and Prospects in India

Table 2-3. *Foodgrain Production, Area, and Yield, India,*
1950–51 to 1977–78

Year	Production (millions of metric tons)	Gross area (millions of hectares)	Yield (kilograms per hectare)	Cropping intensity index[a]
1950–51	50.82	97.32	522	111
1951–52	52.00	96.96	536	112
1952–53	59.20	102.09	580	112
1953–54	69.82	109.06	640	112
1954–55	68.04	107.86	631	113
1955–56	66.85	110.56	605	114
1956–57	69.86	111.14	629	114
1957–58	64.31	109.48	587	113
1958–59	77.14	114.76	672	115
1959–60	76.67	115.82	662	115
1960–61	82.02	115.58	710	115
1961–62	82.71	117.23	705	115
1962–63	80.15	117.84	680	115
1963–64	80.64	117.42	687	115
1964–65	89.36	118.11	757	115
1965–66	72.35	115.10	629	114
1966–67	74.23	115.30	644	115
1967–68	95.05	121.42	783	117
1968–69	94.01	120.43	781	116
1969–70	99.50	123.57	805	117
1970–71	108.42	124.32	872	118
1971–72	105.17	122.62	858	118
1972–73	97.03	119.28	813	118
1973–74	104.66	126.54	827	119
1974–75	99.83	121.08	824	119
1975–76	121.03	128.18	944	120
1976–77	111.17	124.36	894	n.a.
1977–78	125.61	127.13	988	n.a.

Source: Government of India, Ministry of Agriculture and Irrigation, Directorate of Economics and Statistics, *Estimates of Area and Production of Principal Crops in India, 1977–78* (Delhi: Controller of Publications, 1979), table 1, pp. 6–9; cropping intensity index, appendix table A-3.
n.a. Not available.
a. Gross cropped area as percent of net cropped area.

percent of the expansion of the area sown was due to increased double cropping (0.3 percent a year), the remainder being accounted for by the expansion of the net cultivated area (see table 2-3).

CHAPTER THREE

Input Factors Affecting Production

ALTHOUGH the causes of the fluctuations of grain production in India have been the subject of perennial debates, there has been a remarkable dearth of statistical analysis. Whenever production drops or stagnates, as it did in 1965–66 and in 1971–74, critics rush in to blame policies with which they disagree; when things go well, as in 1967–70 and 1975–78, planners and activists are quick to take credit for what they have done or advocated. A question not often addressed, however, is whether the observed crop fluctuations cannot be largely explained by changing weather conditions. Elimination of weather influences, in turn, would facilitate the analysis of the effects of inputs such as irrigation, fertilizer, and high-yielding varieties, as well as of price policies and other factors that affect grain production.

All Cereals[1]

Variations in rainfall are known to be a major determinant of grain yields in India. Both the total amount of rain and its seasonal distribution play a role, though the total amount is the primary factor. To represent the rainfall variable, an index has been constructed following methodology used in a study by the U.S. Agency for International Development (AID) mission to India in the late 1960s.[2]

Multiple regression techniques can be used to estimate the separate

1. Excluding pulses.
2. Ralph W. Cummings, Jr., and S. K. Ray, "1968–69 Foodgrain Production: Relative Contribution of Weather and New Technology," *Economic and Political Weekly*, Review of Agriculture, September 27, 1969, pp. A-163–A-174. See appendix table A-1, below.

21

effects of the various factors affecting yields (rainfall, fertilizer, high-yielding varieties, irrigation) whenever there is sufficient independent variation among the determining factors. However, three factors (fertilizer, high-yielding varieties, and irrigation) were found to be highly inter-correlated. A high degree of intercorrelation impairs the stability of the regression coefficients and, thus, their dependability as indicators 'of the separate influence of each of these factors on yields. For the purposes of this analysis, therefore, we have adopted a single factor, fertilizer use, to serve as a proxy variable representing the package of modern inputs. The results are as follows (figures in parentheses are t-values):

$$(1) \qquad\qquad Y = 211.78 + 5.00x_1 + 12.27x_2,$$
$$\qquad\qquad (6.59) \qquad (13.54)$$
$$\bar{R}^2 = 0.94$$

where

  Y = yield of cereals (kilograms per hectare)
  x_1 = rainfall index for all cereals
  x_2 = fertilizer use (kilograms per hectare).

With equation 1, the observed yields can now be corrected for the effects of weather. The yields that would have been obtained with normal rainfall (index = 100) are shown in table 3-1 (column 5). Now the effects of technology in accelerating the rate of increase in yields can be seen (figure 3-1) beginning in 1967–68, followed by a leveling-off in 1970–71 to 1973–74, with, interestingly, another sharp upward movement beginning in 1974–75 (which was obscured in that year by unfavorable weather).

It is always useful to examine the unexplained residuals (table 3-1, column 3) to see what other factors, not taken into account in the regression, may have played a role. The largest negative residuals occurred in 1966–67, 1971–72, 1972–73, and 1973–74. Except for 1971–72, these were all years of short crops and food shortages. It is possible that in such years there is a particularly strong tendency on the part of individual farmers as well as local and state authorities to underreport yields in order to escape central government procurement. The largest positive unexplained residuals occurred in 1975–76 and 1976–77, which were years of bumper crops and record stocks. At such times, the incentive to underreport is at a minimum, as procurement prices are equal to (and occasionally higher than) free-market prices. Therefore, the possibility cannot be dismissed that the sharp upsurge of weather-adjusted yields in

Figure 3-1. *Actual and Weather-Adjusted Yields, All Cereals, India, 1960–61 to 1977–78*

Yield (kilograms per hectare)

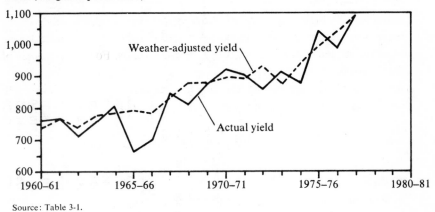

Source: Table 3-1.

1975–78 can be explained, at least in part, by a systematic bias in the crop reports. Production statistics may be expected to be more accurate when food supplies are relatively plentiful.

Other factors may have played a role. The years 1971–72 to 1973–74 saw a sharp decline in the yields of high-yielding varieties of wheat (see table 3-4). This setback was widely attributed to a deterioration in the quality of the seeds and increased susceptibility to wheat rust. Shortages of power to operate irrigation pumps were also reported in 1973–74. In 1975–76, rice production was reported to be favored by an exceptionally good seasonal distribution of rainfall. All this suggests that caution should be used in the interpretation of short-term movements in unadjusted or even weather-adjusted yields.

It is also important to keep in mind that the various types of cereals produced in India are grown under widely varying conditions. Rice, the main cereal, which accounts for about 45 percent of total cereals production, is grown mainly in the monsoon season (summer and fall), mostly in the Ganges and coastal plains. Wheat, which now accounts for nearly 30 percent of total cereals output, is grown mainly in the winter and spring, mostly in the northwest, with a large proportion under irrigation. Coarse grains are grown largely on poorer soils, in upland areas, and without irrigation. Any analysis of total cereals production is, therefore, of rather limited validity.

Table 3-1. Yields and Factors Affecting Yields, All Cereals, India, 1960-61 to 1977-78

| | Yield (kilograms per hectare) | | | | Weather-adjusted yields (kilograms per hectare) | Factors affecting yield | | |
Year	Actual (1)	Estimated (2)	Unexplained residuals[a] (3)	Rainfall index[b] (4)	(5)	Fertilizer consumption[c] (kilograms per hectare) (6)	Area under HYVs[d] (millions of hectares) (7)	Gross irrigated area[e] (millions of hectares) (8)
1960-61	758	749	9	102	748	2.23	...	22.06
1961-62	762	747	15	100	762	2.89	...	22.45
1962-63	716	725	-9	94	746	3.57	...	23.39
1963-64	753	744	9	96	773	4.31	...	23.34
1964-65	810	796	14	105	785	4.84	...	23.94
1965-66	667	652	15	74	797	5.73	...	24.02
1966-67	696	728	-32	83	781	8.27	1.9	25.79
1967-68	849	860	-11	103	834	10.90	6.0	26.10
1968-69	820	801	19	89	875	11.81	9.3	28.05
1969-70	872	874	-2	99	877	13.70	11.4	29.55

Year							
1970–71	920	915	5	104	900	15.00	15.3	30.12
1971–72	908	955	−47	104	888	18.22	18.0	30.54
1972–73	853	871	−21	84	930	19.50	22.3	30.74
1973–74	902	958	−68	103	875	18.89	26.0	31.17
1974–75	874	872	2	87	939	18.38	26.9	33.26
1975–76	1,040	1,001	39	110	990	19.56	30.0	34.08
1976–77	984	950	34	90	1,034	23.55	33.0	n.a.
1977–78	1,098	1,068	30	100	1,098	29.11	35.0	n.a.

Sources: Column 1, Government of India, Ministry of Agriculture and Irrigation, Directorate of Economics and Statistics, *Estimates of Area and Production of Principal Crops in India, 1977–78* (Delhi: Controller of Publications, 1979) (hereafter, *Estimates of Area and Production, 1977–78*), calculated on the basis of index numbers; columns 2 and 5, calculated by equation 1 in text; column 4, Ralph W. Cummings, Jr., and S. K. Ray, "1968–69 Foodgrain Production: Relative Contribution of Weather and New Technology," *Economic and Political Weekly*, Review of Agriculture, September 27, 1969, pp. A-163–A-174, and for 1970–78, authors' calculations (see also appendix table A-1); column 6, authors' calculations based on data from Fertilizer Association of India, *Fertilizer Statistics*, for years shown, and *Estimates of Area and Production, 1977–78*, table 1, pp. 3–5; column 7, *Fertilizer Statistics*, for years shown; column 8, *Estimates of Area and Production*, for years shown.

a. Column 1 − column 2.

b. Three steps are involved in the construction of the rainfall indexes: (1) rainfall reported for thirty-one major divisions were aggregated separately for each season into state averages based on acreage weights; (2) state aggregates were converted into all-India averages based on cereal production in 1959–61; and (3) these were converted into percentages of normal (long-term average) rainfall. For further details see source, above.

c. Assumes 70 percent of total fertilizer is devoted to cereals. Expressed in pure nutrients (NPK).

d. High-yielding varieties.

e. For all foodgrains.

Wheat

Wheat production in India experienced two periods of rapid expansion: in the first half of the 1950s, when production rose by almost 50 percent, and from 1966–67 to 1971–72, when it more than doubled. In the earlier period, this expansion was accomplished mainly by a 40 percent increase in area planted to wheat. In the second period, the expansion was due in equal measure to a 50 percent increase in area and a 50 percent increase in yields (table 3-2).

Table 3-2. *Wheat Production, Area, and Yield, India, 1951–52 to 1977–78*

Year	Production (millions of metric tons)	Gross area (millions of hectares)	Yield (kilograms per hectare)
1951–52	6.34	9.48	669
1952–53	7.61	9.82	775
1953–54	8.10	10.69	758
1954–55	9.15	11.26	813
1955–56	8.87	12.36	718
1956–57	9.50	13.53	702
1957–58	8.00	11.74	681
1958–59	9.95	12.61	789
1959–60	10.33	13.39	771
1960–61	11.00	12.92	851
1961–62	12.07	13.57	889
1962–63	10.78	13.60	793
1963–64	9.85	13.51	729
1964–65	12.26	13.43	913
1965–66	10.40	12.57	827
1966–67	11.40	12.84	888
1967–68	16.55	15.01	1,103
1968–69	17.49	15.96	1,096
1969–70	20.10	16.63	1,209
1970–71	23.84	18.24	1,307
1971–72	26.41	19.13	1,380
1972–73	24.74	19.45	1,272
1973–74	21.78	18.57	1,173
1974–75	24.24	18.09	1,340
1975–76	28.33	20.11	1,409
1976–77	29.00	20.92	1,386
1977–78	31.33	21.20	1,478

Source: *Estimates of Area and Production, 1977–78,* calculated on the basis of index numbers given in the source.

The expansion of the acreage planted to wheat in the late 1960s was a response to two major factors that greatly enhanced the profitability of this crop: rapidly increasing productivity based on the new technology involving high-yielding varieties (HYVs) and increased supplies of water and fertilizer, and favorable weather conditions (appendix table A-1). Beginning in 1972–73, the wheat area leveled off at about 19 million hectares as productivity ceased to increase. In 1975–76 to 1977–78, wheat acreage resumed its upward trend as productivity rose with increased fertilizer use and improved weather conditions.

In analyzing wheat yields, multiple regression techniques are used again to separate the effects of weather and technology. The rainfall index constructed for this purpose is described in appendix table A-1. As in the case of total cereals, fertilizer consumption is used as a proxy representing the entire package of technological inputs (fertilizer, pesticides, water, and high-yielding varieties). Since time series on fertilizer use broken down by crops are not available, use for wheat was estimated by allocating total fertilizer consumption on the basis of a survey conducted by the National Council of Applied Economic Research for 1970–71.[3]

A linear function fitted to data for 1957–58 to 1977–78 gave the following results (figures in parentheses are t-values):

$$(2) \qquad Y = 476.13 + 2.49x_1 + 20.49x_2,$$
$$(2.58) \qquad (16.16)$$
$$\bar{R}^2 = 0.93$$

where

Y = yield in kilograms per hectare

x_1 = rainfall index

x_2 = fertilizer use in kilograms per hectare.

From equation 2 it is now possible to separate the effects of technology from those of weather; the actual wheat yields are adjusted for fluctuations in rainfall by holding the rainfall index constant at 100 in the

3. National Council of Applied Economic Research, *Fertilizer Use on Selected Crops in India* (New Delhi: NCAER and the Fertilizer Association of India, 1974). The survey indicates that farmers in 1970–71 were using 19.2 and 31.4 percent of total NPK on wheat and rice, respectively (p. 37). Since most of the fertilizer is used on irrigated land, we have estimated fertilizer use in other years on the basis of changes in the percentage share of wheat and rice, respectively, in the gross irrigated area in each year. The ratios of irrigated area under wheat and rice to total gross irrigated area in 1970–71 were 25.5 percent and 38.7 percent, respectively.

equation. The weather-adjusted yields are shown in table 3-3, column 2, together with estimated fertilizer consumption (column 3), yields as estimated from rainfall and fertilizer use (column 4), and the residuals not explained by rainfall and fertilizer use (column 5).

Table 3-3. *Actual and Weather-Adjusted Yields, Fertilizer Consumption, and Unexplained Residuals, Wheat, India, 1957–58 to 1977–78*
Kilograms per hectare

Year	Actual yield (1)	Weather-adjusted yield (2)	Fertilizer consumption[a] (3)	Estimated yield (4)	Unexplained residuals[b] (5)
1957–58	681	724	1.74	718	−37
1958–59	789	795	2.00	761	28
1959–60	771	738	2.67	813	−42
1960–61	851	795	2.59	835	16
1961–62	889	814	2.86	859	30
1962–63	793	796	3.91	803	−10
1963–64	729	720	4.83	833	−104
1964–65	913	868	6.99	907	6
1965–66	827	911	8.23	809	18
1966–67	888	932	12.12	929	−41
1967–68	1,103	1,059	15.05	1,077	26
1968–69	1,096	1,134	18.23	1,060	36
1969–70	1,209	1,210	20.74	1,148	61
1970–71	1,307	1,303	23.75	1,215	92
1971–72	1,380	1,345	27.83	1,329	51
1972–73	1,272	1,327	29.54	1,274	−2
1973–74	1,173	1,161	30.77	1,366	−193
1974–75	1,340	1,397	28.63	1,253	87
1975–76	1,409	1,383	28.96	1,343	66
1976–77	1,386	1,380	32.82	1,402	−16
1977–78	1,478	1,488	40.90	1,550	−72

Sources: Column 1, *Estimates of Area and Production, 1977–78*, calculated on the basis of index numbers of yields; columns 2 and 4, calculated by equation 2 in text; column 3, estimated from Fertilizer Association of India, *Fertilizer Statistics*, for years shown, based on National Council of Applied Economic Research, *Fertilizer Use on Selected Crops in India* (New Delhi: NCAER and the Fertilizer Association of India, 1974).
a. Expressed in pure nutrients (NPK).
b. Column 1 − column 4.

As can be seen from figure 3-2, weather-adjusted yields increased by about 85 percent between 1963–64 and 1971–72; this is the measure of the "green revolution" in wheat. The nearly sixfold increase in fertilizer use was a major factor, but large positive residuals in five successive years (1967–68 to 1971–72) indicate that other factors, reinforcing the ef-

Figure 3-2. *Weather-Adjusted Yields, Fertilizer Consumption, and Unexplained Residuals, Wheat, India, 1957–58 to 1977–78*

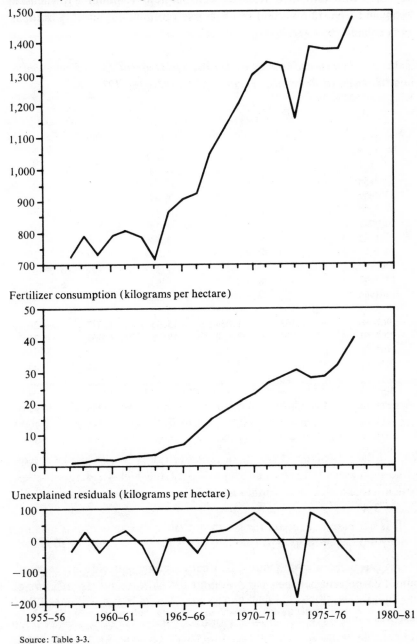

Weather-adjusted yield (kilograms per hectare)

Fertilizer consumption (kilograms per hectare)

Unexplained residuals (kilograms per hectare)

Source: Table 3-3.

fects of fertilizer, were at work during that period. This was also the period when the HYVs were introduced: the percentage of the wheat acreage planted to HYVs rose from 4 percent in 1966–67 to 41 percent in 1971–72 (table 3-4).

Table 3-4. *Percent of Area under HYVs, Yields of HYVs, and Percent Irrigated, Wheat, India, 1966–67 to 1977–78*

Year	Percent under HYVs	Yields of HYVs (kilograms per hectare)	Percent irrigated
1966–67	4.2	n.a.	47.7
1967–68	19.6	n.a.	43.1
1968–69	30.0	2,333	48.7
1969–70	29.6	2,481	51.8
1970–71	35.8	2,407	53.9
1971–72	41.1	2,135	54.0
1972–73	51.4	1,739	55.2
1973–74	59.3	1,440	57.8
1974–75	61.9	1,524	61.6
1975–76	62.1	1,537	61.9[a]
1976–77	69.4	n.a.	n.a.
1977–78	73.3	n.a.	n.a.

Sources: Area under HYVs, Fertilizer Association of India, *Fertilizer Statistics*, for years shown; *Estimates of Area and Production, 1977–78*, table 1, pp. 3–5, and preceding issues. HYV yields, unpublished data provided by U.S. Department of Agriculture, Foreign Agricultural Service, Office of the Agricultural Attaché, New Delhi.
n.a. Not available.
a. Preliminary.

Beginning in 1971–72 and continuing through 1976–77, the trend of weather-adjusted yields leveled off. This may be traced, in the main, to two developments: a temporary leveling-off in fertilizer use because of tight supplies caused by the cautious import policies in 1972–73 and 1973–74 and the subsequent doubling of fertilizer prices in the wake of the oil price increase;[4] and the declining yields of the high-yielding varieties, which largely offset the continuing growth in the area planted to HYVs (table 3-4).

It is not easy to account for the extent and abruptness of this decline, from 2.5 tons per hectare in 1969–70 to 1.5 tons per hectare in 1974–75.

4. See Gunvant M. Desai, "A Critical Review of Fertilizer Consumption after 1974–75 and Prospects for Future Growth," *Fertilizer News*, vol. 23 (July 1978), pp. 7–18; see also chapter 4, below. Compare also Dharm Narain, "Growth of Productivity in Indian Agriculture," *Indian Journal of Agricultural Economics*, vol. 32 (January–March 1977), pp. 1–44; and A. Vaidyanathan, "Performance and Prospects of Crop Production in India," *Economic and Political Weekly*, special number (August 1977), pp. 1355–68.

To be sure, a gradual decline could be expected as HYVs began to be planted on less fertile land or on land with less dependable rainfall or irrigation. Indeed, irrigation may have become an effective constraint on further improvements in wheat yields. As can be seen from table 3-4, the expansion of the irrigated wheat acreage, although quite rapid, did not keep up with the even more rapid expansion of the area under HYVs; by 1973–74, the wheat area under HYVs had caught up with the irrigated area. Moreover, irrigation is not equally reliable from year to year where it depends on rainfall and river flows; thus insufficient rainfall curtailed canal irrigation in some areas in 1972–73. Since the HYVs require a dependable water supply, any further benefits to be gained from the HYVs will require not only further expansion of the area under irrigation, but also improvements in the dependability of the existing irrigation facilities. Declining fertilizer doses on HYVs, as their use spread among farmers less able, or more reluctant, to purchase adequate quantities, may also have played a role. Small farmers, in particular, find it difficult to obtain credit for this purpose.[5]

It was always recognized that the "miracle seeds" could reach their full potential only as part of a package that includes adequate supplies of water and fertilizer. But experience in Mexico and elsewhere[6] also suggests that specific strains tend to run into problems and have to be replaced by other strains better adapted to their environment. Thus the new varieties—particularly the Kalyan Sona variety, which accounts for the major portion of the wheat acreage planted to HYVs—were found to be susceptible to leaf and strife rust. Severe rust damage seems to have been a major factor in the sharp drop in yields in 1973–74 (which cannot be explained by weather conditions or fertilizer availability).[7] Unfavorable prices may also have played a role.[8] There are indications, moreover, that poor seed quality has become a problem.[9]

5. See chapter 5.
6. See Dana G. Dalrymple and William I. Jones, "Evaluating the 'Green Revolution,'" paper prepared for joint meeting of the American Association for the Advancement of Science and the Consejo Nacional de Ciencia y Technologia, Mexico City, June 20, 1973.
7. Government of India, *Economic Survey, 1974–75* (New Delhi: Government of India Press, 1975), p. 7.
8. See chapter 4.
9. Wolf Ladejinsky, "How Green Is the Indian Green Revolution?" *Economic and Political Weekly*, Review of Agriculture, December 29, 1973, pp. A-133–A-144; M. S. Swaminathan, "Our Agricultural Future," Sardar Patel Memorial Lecture, New Delhi, October 1973; Government of India, Agricultural Prices Commission, "Report on Price Policy for Wheat for the 1975–76 Season," February 1975.

To sum up, the lack of progress in wheat yields after 1971–72 can be explained essentially as a result of: the leveling-off of fertilizer use; the limitations of existing irrigation facilities; and problems with seed quality and disease resistance of the HYVs. The sharp decline in yields of HYVs in 1973–74 can probably be attributed in large part to rust damage in that year.

There are indications that the factors responsible for the stagnation of wheat yields after 1971–72 are being corrected. Research on new high-yielding varieties has been stepped up. New disease-resistant seeds are being tried on a limited scale. Although no specific data on irrigated area under individual crops are available after 1975–76, it is clear from the plan document, *Draft Five Year Plan, 1978–83,* that the growth in irrigated area accelerated during the Fifth Plan period.[10] Most important, fertilizer use has resumed its upward trend. While it is too early to draw definite conclusions, the significant rise in weather-adjusted wheat yields in 1977–78 (figure 3-2) is encouraging.

Rice

Though rice production in India has been growing more slowly than that of wheat, production nonetheless has doubled since 1951–52. About one-third of this growth can be attributed to the expansion of gross area, the remainder to the increase in yields. During this period, the rate of expansion of the gross area planted to rice has been declining, from about 1.5 percent annually in the 1950s to 1 percent in the 1960s and 0.8 percent in the 1970s. Yields have risen at an average rate of 1.5 percent, but there was little growth in the sixties and early seventies (table 3-5).

As in the case of wheat, the effects of weather and technology on rice yields can be separated by means of a regression analysis involving a rainfall index[11] and fertilizer use, representing the package of technological inputs (fertilizer, pesticides, water, and high-yielding varieties).[12] The

10. Government of India, Planning Commission, *Draft Five Year Plan, 1978–83* (Delhi: Controller of Publications, 1978).

11. See appendix table A-1.

12. Fertilizer use on rice was estimated in the same manner as for wheat. See footnote 3 to this chapter.

Table 3-5. *Rice Production, Area, and Yield, India, 1951–52 to 1977–78*

Year	Production (millions of metric tons)	Gross area (millions of hectares)	Yield (kilograms per hectare)
1951–52	22.59	29.90	755
1952–53	24.29	30.04	809
1953–54	29.76	31.37	949
1954–55	26.53	30.79	862
1955–56	28.64	31.54	908
1956–57	30.20	32.26	936
1957–58	26.53	32.30	821
1958–59	32.00	33.15	965
1959–60	31.80	33.94	937
1960–61	34.58	34.15	1,013
1961–62	35.53	34.56	1,028
1962–63	33.36	35.79	932
1963–64	36.99	35.80	1,033
1964–65	39.30	36.45	1,078
1965–66	30.57	35.41	863
1966–67	30.45	35.20	865
1967–68	37.61	36.37	1,034
1968–69	39.58	36.88	1,073
1969–70	40.25	37.60	1,070
1970–71	42.06	37.50	1,120
1971–72	43.14	37.91	1,138
1972–73	39.30	36.83	1,067
1973–74	44.13	38.25	1,153
1974–75	40.32	37.90	1,064
1975–76	49.46	39.69	1,246
1976–77	41.92	38.51	1,088
1977–78	52.68	40.00	1,317

Source: *Estimates of Area and Production, 1977–78*, calculated on the basis of index numbers given in the source.

function fitted to the data for 1957–58 to 1977–78 gave the following results (figures in parentheses are t-values):

$$(3) \qquad Y = 277.80 + 6.67x_1 + 7.31x_2,$$
$$(6.23) \qquad (6.15)$$
$$\bar{R}^2 = 0.87$$

where

Y = yield in kilograms per hectare

x_1 = rainfall index

x_2 = fertilizer use in kilograms per hectare.

Figure 3-3. *Weather-Adjusted Yields, Fertilizer Consumption, and Unexplained Residuals, Rice, India, 1957–58 to 1977–78*

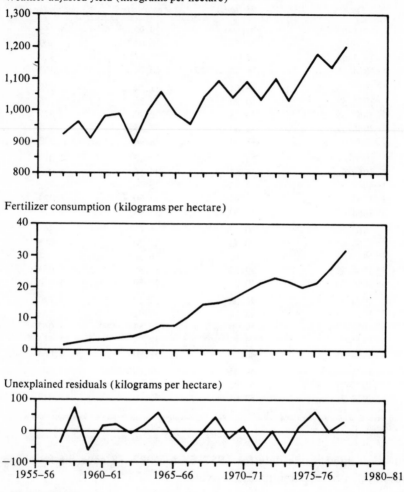

Weather-adjusted yield (kilograms per hectare)

Fertilizer consumption (kilograms per hectare)

Unexplained residuals (kilograms per hectare)

Source: Table 3-6.

From equation 3 it is possible to calculate the weather-adjusted yields (table 3-6, column 2), the yields that can be estimated from rainfall and fertilizer use (column 4), and the residuals that remain unexplained (column 5). As can be seen from figure 3-3, the weather-adjusted yields increased at a more or less steady rate of about 1.3 percent throughout the period. The acceleration in fertilizer use during the period 1965–66 to

Table 3-6. *Actual and Weather-Adjusted Yields, Fertilizer Consumption, and Unexplained Residuals, Rice, India, 1957–58 to 1977–78*
Kilograms per hectare

Year	Actual yield (1)	Weather-adjusted yield (2)	Fertilizer consumption[a] (3)	Estimated yield (4)	Unexplained residuals[b] (5)
1957–58	821	924	2.04	857	−36
1958–59	965	962	2.45	889	76
1959–60	937	915	3.24	990	−53
1960–61	1,013	978	3.15	1,003	10
1961–62	1,028	983	3.62	1,016	12
1962–63	932	889	4.68	935	−3
1963–64	1,033	996	5.51	1,021	12
1964–65	1,078	1,060	7.62	1,018	60
1965–66	863	980	7.51	883	−20
1966–67	865	950	10.40	935	−70
1967–68	1,034	1,046	14.34	1,037	−3
1968–69	1,073	1,097	15.00	1,030	43
1969–70	1,070	1,045	16.79	1,090	−20
1970–71	1,120	1,092	18.85	1,110	10
1971–72	1,138	1,040	21.53	1,199	−61
1972–73	1,063	1,108	22.69	1,064	−1
1973–74	1,153	1,038	22.05	1,221	−68
1974–75	1,064	1,109	20.25	1,047	17
1975–76	1,246	1,174	21.92	1,176	70
1976–77	1,088	1,139	26.56	1,087	1
1977–78	1,317	1,208	32.39	1,290	27

Sources: Column 1, same as table 3-3, column 1; columns 2 and 4, calculated from equation 3 in text; column 3, same as table 3-3, column 3.
a. Expressed in pure nutrients (NPK).
b. Column 1 − column 4.

1971–72 did not lead to a noticeable acceleration in the trend of weather-adjusted yields. The residuals are random, suggesting that the high-yielding varieties had no significant impact on rice yields in India.

What are the reasons for the limited impact of the new technology on rice yields? First, it should be noted that modern inputs are not applied as extensively to rice as to wheat. Fertilizer use, the percentage of area under HYVs, and the percentage irrigated are all lower than for wheat:

	Year	Rice	Wheat
Fertilizer use (kilograms NPK per hectare)	1976–77	26.6	32.8
Percent of area under HYVs	1976–77	34.6	69.4
Percent of area irrigated	1973–74	38.4	57.8

Table 3-7. *Area under HYVs and Area Irrigated, Rice, India.*
1966–67 to 1977–78
Percent

Year	Area under HYVs	Area irrigated
1966–67	2.5	37.9
1967–68	4.9	38.0
1968–69	7.0	37.1
1969–70	11.3	38.9
1970–71	14.5	39.7
1971–72	19.1	38.7
1972–73	22.1	39.4
1973–74	26.1	38.4
1974–75	28.6	38.8
1975–76	31.5	37.9[a]
1976–77	34.6	n.a.
1977–78	38.8	n.a.

Sources: Fertilizer Association of India, *Fertilizer Statistics*, for years shown; and *Estimates of Area and Production, 1977–78*, table 1, pp. 3–5, and preceding issues.
n.a. Not available.
a. Estimate.

However, fertilizer use (table 3-6, column 3) and the area under HYVs (table 3-7) did increase substantially. Why was this not reflected in an increased rate of growth of rice yields?

A major factor is the much lower response ratio of rice yields to fertilizer use (7.3, as compared with 20.5 for wheat).[13] This is especially true for the traditional varieties, which tend to convert a large part of additional nutrients into stem and leaf growth rather than seeds. This tendency is abetted by the climate of the monsoon season (June to October), during which 95 percent of the rice in India is grown. Cloudy days and warm nights favor the growth of leaves and shoots, which consume the greater part of photosynthates and leave little for root and grain growth.

The HYVs introduced thus far did not overcome this climatic handicap. They proved to be much better adapted to the climatic conditions of the dry season, when bright days and cool nights tend to favor grain and root growth over that of leaves and shoots.[14] A comparison of annual rates

13. From equations 3 and 2.
14. J. Papadakis, *The Food Problem of India: And the Related Problems of Industrial Development, Investment and Inflation* (Rome: J. Papadakis, 1967).

of growth of rice yields in different seasons, 1967–68 to 1969–70 and 1975–76 to 1977–78, will illustrate this point:

Season	Annual growth rate (percent)
Wet	1.6
Dry	2.9
Average	1.7

The higher rates of growth in the dry season can probably be traced to the preference of the HYVs for these particular climatic conditions. In parts of South India, West Bengal, and Bihar, HYV rice is now being increasingly grown in the dry season. However, since the summer rice area is only 4.5 percent of the total, its effect on national rice yields is thus far insignificant.

Equally important are the deficiencies of the Indian irrigation system. The new technology requires an adequate and well-regulated water supply. Not only are the HYVs extremely sensitive to water shortages, they also are more vulnerable to flood conditions than the traditional varieties, whose stems are longer and capable of adapting to the water level. The existing irrigation system falls far short of meeting these requirements. Less than 40 percent of the rice area is irrigated, as compared with 60 percent for wheat. Also in contrast to wheat, the percentage of the rice area under irrigation hardly increased between 1966–67 and 1975–76 (table 3-7).

Moreover, much of the irrigation is undependable. In many rice-growing regions, water supplies are derived solely from diversion of unregulated rivers that depend entirely on monsoon rains, as in Central and Peninsular India. The supply available for irrigation, therefore, varies with the river flow. In addition, most of the major and medium-size irrigation projects in India are overextended, so as to provide relief in dry years to as large an area as possible. This means spreading the water thinly, with resulting evaporation and seepage losses, rather than ensuring an adequate water supply at all times to a more limited area of intensive cultivation. Hence, many of the existing irrigation works, which were giving creditable performances at the time they were constructed, are now proving inadequate to meet the exacting requirements of the high-yielding varieties.[15] This again is in contrast to wheat, which is grown in the dry

15. Government of India, Ministry of Irrigation and Power, *Report of the Irrigation Commission, 1972*, vol. 1 (Faridabad, Haryana, India: Thomson Press [India] Ltd., for the Ministry, 1972).

season and receives irrigation either through groundwater sources or through reservoirs where water can be stored. In either case, the supply of water can, by and large, be controlled and regulated to meet the specific requirements of the crop.

The record crops of rice in 1975–76 to 1977–78 still lack a fully adequate explanation. Favorable weather accounts for part of it. But weather-adjusted yields in these years averaged 1,174 kilograms per hectare, about 100 kilograms more than the average level of the seven preceding years (table 3-6, column 2). The 1975–76 crop was favored by the fact that rainfall in that year was not only adequate in quantity but also timely and well-distributed over the season. In 1976–77 and 1977–78, the sharp increase in fertilizer use played a significant role. Finally, there are indications, as mentioned earlier, that irrigation development has accelerated in recent years.

What conclusions can be drawn from past experience? Increased fertilizer use is necessary, but it alone will not provide the answer. Improved water control will be essential for raising rice yields in the wet season. New varieties must be developed that are better adapted to the climatic conditions of the monsoon season. And the cultivation of irrigated rice can be increased in the dry season, which seems to provide favorable conditions for the existing HYVs.

Coarse Grains

Coarse grains[16] were planted on 34 percent of the foodgrain area in 1975–76 to 1977–78 but accounted for less than 25 percent of the production and 14 percent of the fertilizer used on foodgrains (1970–71). Since coarse grains are generally grown in less fertile areas and on non-irrigated land, yields are lower than for rice and wheat. Moreover, yields and production of coarse grains have generally stagnated or declined (table 3-8).

The reasons for this are both technological and economic. Dependence on rainfall involves high risks that discourage the use of modern technology. The spread of HYVs has been very slow (accounting for 15 percent of the gross area in 1976–77, as compared with 69 percent for wheat and 35 percent for rice) and it is largely confined to areas with

16. Coarse grains are defined here as total foodgrains minus wheat, rice, and pulses; this includes maize, sorghum, millet, and other minor coarse grains.

assured rainfall and other favorable agroclimatic conditions. The HYVs are susceptible to diseases such as ergot and downy mildew on millets and shootfly and mold on sorghum, and this has contributed to low profitability and high risks.[17] The consumption of coarse grains is mainly confined to low-income groups, and their prices are low relative to other cereals. Also, prices tend to fall sharply in years of ample supply.[18]

As a result of these conditions, coarse grains are accorded a low priority in the farmers' production planning. Whenever land is brought under irrigation, coarse grains tend to be replaced by more profitable crops. The solution to the problems of coarse grains lies in the evolution of a low-cost dry-farming technology. Any major increase in the production of coarse grains in India is unlikely until such a technological breakthrough is achieved.

Pulses

The poor production performance of pulses (table 3-8) is surprising in view of their importance as a source of protein in the Indian diet. The main reason is their low profitability relative to competing cereals. Pulse yields have stagnated at low levels while wheat yields, in particular, increased rapidly. As a result, land previously planted to pulses has been shifted to wheat wherever possible.[19]

Contrary to what one might expect, the demand was not strong enough to raise prices sufficiently to induce growers to expand the area planted to pulses.[20] In the marketplace, pulses were at a disadvantage in competing with wheat for the limited purchasing power of India's poor. At low levels of calorie intake, wheat is a better bargain. The cost advantage

17. S. L. Bapna, "Production of Coarse Cereals in India: Past Performance and Future Prospects" (Hyderabad, India: International Crops Research Institute for the Semi-Arid Tropics, December 1976), p. 36.

18. Thus Jodha points out that when the adoption of hybrid seeds led to increased production of millets in Rajasthan and Gujarat, prices crashed in 1969–70 and many producers dropped out of the program. See N. S. Jodha, "Prospects for Coarse Cereals: Permanent Constraints of Jowar and Bajra," *Economic and Political Weekly*, Review of Agriculture, December 29, 1973, pp. A-145–A-150.

19. See B. L. Kumar, "Declining Trend in Production of Pulses and Factors Affecting It," *Economic and Political Weekly*, July 8, 1978, pp. 1112–14.

20. This despite the fact that in the 1960s the real price of pulses rose substantially more (30 percent) than that of cereals (about 10 percent).

Table 3-8. Area,[a] Production,[b] and Yield[c] of Major Coarse Grains and Pulses, India, 1950–51 to 1977–78

Year	Maize			Sorghum			Millet			Pulses		
	Area	Production	Yield	Area	Production	Yield	Area	Production	Yield	Area	Production	Yield
1950–51	3.2	1.7	547	15.6	5.5	353	9.0	2.6	288	19.1	8.4	441
1951–52	3.3	2.1	627	15.9	6.1	381	9.5	2.3	246	18.8	8.4	448
1952–53	3.6	2.9	796	17.5	7.4	420	10.8	3.2	296	19.8	9.2	463
1953–54	3.9	3.0	785	17.8	8.1	455	12.2	4.5	373	21.7	10.6	489
1954–55	3.7	3.0	794	17.5	9.2	527	11.4	3.5	310	21.9	11.0	500
1955–56	3.7	2.6	704	17.4	6.7	387	11.3	3.4	302	23.2	11.0	476
1956–57	3.8	3.1	819	16.2	7.3	451	11.3	2.9	255	23.3	11.6	495
1957–58	4.1	3.2	772	17.3	8.6	499	11.2	3.6	324	22.5	9.6	424
1958–59	4.3	3.5	812	18.0	9.0	503	11.4	3.9	338	24.3	13.1	541
1959–60	4.3	4.1	938	17.7	8.6	484	10.7	3.5	327	24.8	11.8	475
1960–61	4.4	4.1	926	18.4	9.8	533	11.5	3.3	286	23.6	12.7	539
1961–62	4.5	4.3	957	18.2	8.0	440	11.3	3.6	323	24.2	11.6	485
1962–63	4.6	4.6	992	18.4	9.7	529	11.0	4.0	361	24.3	11.5	475
1963–64	4.6	4.6	995	18.4	9.2	501	11.1	3.9	349	24.2	10.1	416
1964–65	4.6	4.7	1,010	18.1	9.7	536	11.8	4.5	382	23.9	12.4	520

	a	b	c	a	b	c	a	b	c	a	b	c
1965–66	4.8	4.8	1,005	17.7	7.6	429	12.0	3.8	314	22.7	9.9	438
1966–67	5.1	4.9	964	18.1	9.2	511	12.2	4.5	365	22.1	8.3	377
1967–68	5.6	6.3	1,123	18.4	10.0	545	12.8	5.2	405	22.6	12.1	534
1968–69	5.7	5.7	997	18.7	9.8	523	12.1	3.8	315	21.3	10.4	490
1969–70	5.9	5.7	968	18.6	9.7	522	12.5	5.3	426	22.0	11.7	531
1970–71	5.8	7.5	1,279	17.4	8.1	466	12.9	8.0	622	22.5	11.8	524
1971–72	5.7	5.1	900	16.8	7.7	460	11.8	5.3	452	22.2	11.1	501
1972–73	5.8	6.4	1,094	15.5	7.0	449	11.8	3.9	333	20.9	9.9	474
1973–74	6.0	5.8	965	16.7	9.1	544	13.9	7.5	540	23.4	10.0	427
1974–75	5.9	5.6	948	16.2	10.4	643	11.3	3.3	290	22.0	10.0	455
1975–76	6.0	7.3	1,203	16.1	9.5	591	11.6	5.7	496	24.5	13.0	533
1976–77	6.0	6.4	1,060	15.8	10.5	667	10.8	5.9	544	23.0	11.4	494
1977–78	5.7	5.9	1,043	16.3	11.8	726	11.0	4.7	427	23.5	11.8	501

Source: Government of India, Ministry of Agriculture and Irrigation, Directorate of Economics and Statistics, *Estimates of Area and Production of Principal Crops, 1977–78* (Delhi: Controller of Publications, 1979), table 1, pp. 2–9. Figures are rounded.

a. Millions of hectares.
b. Millions of metric tons.
c. Kilograms per hectare.

of wheat was enhanced further by government price controls that applied to wheat but not to pulses.[21]

Given the yield differential, shifting land from pulses to wheat is defensible from a nutritional standpoint because it increases the total supply of nutrients available to the population, including protein.[22] Nevertheless, there is reason to expect that the demand for pulses will increase significantly once more people are able to satisfy their minimum calorie requirements and have something left over to spend on high-protein foods. Among the latter, pulses are the best value. Pulses are also useful in crop rotation because of their ability to fix nitrogen—an important advantage in an era of high energy prices.

There is justification, therefore, for current efforts to raise productivity and reduce the costs of pulse production. Yields may be increased by closer spacing where conditions are favorable. The area may be expanded by double-cropping after wheat, or on rice fallows. In the long run, the development of higher yielding varieties is the best hope for increased production.[23]

21. The following example illustrates the price advantage of wheat. In 1973–74, one kilogram of whole wheat flour could be purchased in urban fair-price shops at slightly over half the price of one kilo of dried pulses (1.46 rupees vs. 2.61 rupees) (authors' calculations based on the National Sample Survey, which is taken annually by the government of India). The wheat flour supplies the same number of calories and about half the amount of protein.

22. See James G. Ryan and M. Asokan, "Effect of Green Revolution in Wheat on Production of Pulses and Nutrients in India," *Indian Journal of Agricultural Economics,* vol. 32 (July–September 1977), pp. 8–15.

23. Government of India, Ministry of Agriculture and Irrigation, Department of Agricultural Research and Education, *Report, 1977–78* (New Delhi: Government of India Press, 1978), p. 37.

CHAPTER FOUR

Economic Factors

THERE IS a widespread view, particularly among American economists, that prices received by the Indian farmer are not high enough to provide adequate incentives to increase foodgrain production and that lack of profitability has been a factor in the disappointing performance in certain periods. In particular, food import policy (including food aid) and the Indian foodgrain procurement system have been singled out for criticism. Indian stock management has also been questioned.

To keep the matter in perspective, it is important to realize that providing adequate incentives for domestic food production is only one—albeit the most important—of several objectives of Indian food policy. Other major objectives are price stabilization and the assurance of a minimum level of nutrition for the urban poor. Thus Indian policies must be examined in the light of these objectives.

Imports and Stock Management

Government management of imports and stocks has been criticized because of its failure actually to stabilize supplies and prices.[1] While this criticism is justified, it is nevertheless clear from the evidence that government intervention has generally been in the right direction. With few exceptions, the combined effect of import and stock policy (table 4-1, column 5) has been in the opposite direction from fluctuations in domestic foodgrain production (column 1).

1. See, for example, Raj Krishna, "Government Operations in Foodgrains," *Economic and Political Weekly,* September 16, 1967, pp. 1695–1706; John Wall, "Foodgrain Management: Pricing, Procurement, Distribution, Import and Storage Policy," in *India: Occasional Papers,* World Bank Staff Working Paper 279 (World Bank, 1978), pp. 43–91, particularly table 3; Shlomo Reutlinger, "The Level and Stability of India's Foodgrain Consumption," in *India: Occasional Papers,* pp. 92–123. It should be noted, however, that the available data on stock operations do not include changes in private stocks.

Table 4-1. Foodgrain Production Shortfalls, Releases from Stocks, and Net Imports, India, 1960–61 to 1977–78
Millions of metric tons

| | Foodgrain production (deviations from trend) (1) | Releases from stocks[a] (2) | Net imports | | Net imports plus releases from stocks[b] (5) | Foodgrain supply[c] (6) |
Year			Total (3)	Deviations from average (4)		
1960–61	6.9	0.2	3.5	−1.3	−1.1	5.8
1961–62	5.5	0.4	3.6	−1.2	−0.8	4.7
1962–63	0.8	0.0	4.5	−0.3	−0.3	0.6
1963–64	−0.9	1.2	6.3	1.5	2.7	1.8
1964–65	5.6	−1.1	7.4	2.6	1.5	7.2
1965–66	−13.7	−0.1	10.3	5.5	5.4	−8.3
1966–67	−14.3	0.3	8.7	3.9	4.2	−10.1
1967–68	4.2	−2.0	5.7	0.9	−1.1	3.1
1968–69	0.5	−0.5	3.8	−1.0	−1.5	−0.9
1969–70	3.4	−1.1	3.5	−1.3	−2.4	1.1
1970–71	9.7	−2.6	2.0	−2.8	−5.4	4.3
1971–72	3.8	4.7	−0.5	−5.3	−0.6	3.2
1972–73	−7.3	0.3	3.6	−1.2	−0.9	−8.2
1973–74	−2.4	0.4	4.8	0.0	0.4	−2.0
1974–75	−10.3	−5.6	7.4	2.6	−3.0	−13.3
1975–76	7.8	−10.6	6.4	1.6	−9.0	−0.9
1976–77	−5.1	1.5	0.4	−4.4	−2.9	−8.2
1977–78	6.5	−0.1	−1.0	−5.8	−5.9	0.6

Sources: Column 1, authors' calculations (see fig. 2-1). Columns 2 and 3, Government of India, Ministry of Agriculture and Irrigation, Directorate of Economics and Statistics, *Bulletin on Food Statistics, 1978*, 28th issue (Delhi: Controller of Publications, 1979), table 11, p. 126.
a. Minus (−) represents additions to stocks.
b. Column 2 + column 4.
c. Column 1 + column 5.

The evidence does not support the thesis that imports and stock management have disrupted the domestic market. Only in one year (1964–65) was above-average production compounded by above-average imports that were not entirely offset by additions to stocks; but even in that year, the effect of government intervention was minor. On the other hand, in three years (1972–73, 1974–75, and 1976–77) crop shortfalls were compounded by stock accumulation or below-average imports, or both.

It can be argued, of course, that the fact that India is importing food at all has a depressing effect on producer prices. No doubt, food prices would be higher in the absence of imports. The impact of a no-import policy would be felt most heavily by low-income groups.[2] To maintain a minimum level of nutrition in the cities, the government would be forced to resort to increased government procurement. In these circumstances, any gains to producers from higher open-market prices would be largely erased by increased mandatory deliveries at controlled prices. The case for food imports is even more persuasive to the extent that imports are made available on concessional terms or as outright grants (see chapter 9).

Indian stock management has become a subject of controversy because of the unprecedented buildup in 1976 and 1977, when government stocks jumped from 8 million tons to 22 million tons. While stocks of this size can be justified if overriding priority is given to a national reserve adequate to meet a worst-case contingency like that experienced in the mid-sixties, there are more cost-effective ways of assuring food security (see chapter 9). The Indian government may have come to the same conclusion. There are reasons to believe that the buildup was the result of a coincidence of unforeseen events: the late arrival of imports ordered in the poor crop year 1974–75 and the succession of record crops in the following three years. The government has already taken steps to reduce these stocks. Imports have been cut; a Soviet grain loan has been repaid in kind; food-for-work projects have been stepped up; and domestic grain consumption has been allowed to rise moderately in the past three years.

Government Procurement and Distribution

Government procurement and distribution of foodgrains at controlled prices dates back to the colonial period. The quantities procured increased

2. See John W. Mellor, "Food Price Policy and Income Distribution in Low-Income Countries," *Economic Development and Cultural Change*, vol. 27 (October 1978), table 4, p. 12.

from about 1 percent of production in the early 1960s to over 5 percent in the drought years 1965–66 and 1966–67. In the 1970s they have varied between 6 and 11 percent of production. Quantities distributed by the system (which includes imports and releases from government stocks) rose from about 5 to 6 percent of total net supplies in the early 1960s to a peak of 19 percent in the mid-sixties, and have recently fluctuated between 9 and 12 percent (table 4-2).

The bulk of foodgrains procured by the government comes from a few surplus areas; in recent years, Punjab and Haryana alone accounted for about half of total foodgrains and almost three-fourths of the wheat.[3] Procurement may be made from rice millers or traders or directly from farmers large enough to have a significant marketable surplus. The methods of procurement have varied a great deal, ranging from requisitioning, levies,[4] and preemptive purchases when supplies are tight to open-market purchases when supplies are ample.[5]

Distribution is made through a network of fair-price shops to registered households on the basis of ration cards. In theory, everyone is entitled to a ration; in practice, the location of the shops—mainly in low-income urban neighborhoods—and the quality of the grains sold ensure that distribution is made mainly to the poor.

To facilitate procurement of grain from surplus areas, the government has from time to time imposed restrictions on the movement of grains from one food zone to another.[6] Zoning bottles up grain in surplus areas and depresses market prices, making it possible for the government to procure at or only slightly above market prices. But the system also causes open-market prices in deficit areas to be higher than they would be in the absence of zoning.[7]

The economic effects of the system are not easy to sort out. In the

3. Wall, "Foodgrain Management," table 2, p. 90.
4. Graded levies on traders and rice millers seem to be the most common practice.
5. An experiment with nationalization of the grain trade in 1973 was quickly abandoned.
6. A food zone generally coincides with a state, though some zones include several states or only part of a state. At present there are no restrictions on the movement of grains from one zone to another.
7. For an excellent description of the system, see Wall, "Foodgrain Management," pp. 52–59. For a critical but inconclusive analysis, see Jagdish N. Bhagwati and Sukhamoy Chakravarty, "Contributions to Indian Economic Analysis: A Survey," *American Economic Review,* vol. 59 (September 1969), pt. 2: Supplement, pp. 1–73.

Table 4-2. *Indian Government Procurement and Distribution of Foodgrains, 1960–61 to 1977–78*
Millions of metric tons unless otherwise specified

Year	Production (1)	Procurement[a] (2)	Procurement as percent of production (3)	Net imports plus releases from stocks (4)	Quantities distributed[a]		Net foodgrain supply	
					Amount (5)	Percent of supply (6)	Total amount[b] (7)	Per capita (kilograms) (8)
1960–61	82.0	1.3	1.6	3.7	4.9	6.5	75.4	171
1961–62	82.7	0.5	0.6	4.0	4.0	5.2	76.4	168
1962–63	80.2	0.5	0.6	4.5	4.4	5.9	74.7	162
1963–64	80.6	0.8	1.0	7.5	5.2	6.7	78.0	165
1964–65	89.4	1.4	1.6	6.3	8.7	10.3	84.5	175
1965–66	72.4	4.0	5.5	10.2	10.1	13.7	73.6	149
1966–67	74.2	4.0	5.4	9.0	14.1	19.1	73.9	146
1967–68	95.1	4.5	4.7	3.7	13.2	15.2	86.9	168
1968–69	94.0	6.8	7.2	3.3	10.2	11.9	85.6	162
1969–70	99.5	6.4	6.4	2.4	9.4	10.5	89.6	166
1970–71	108.4	6.7	6.2	-0.6	8.8	9.3	94.2	171
1971–72	105.2	8.9	8.5	4.2	7.8	8.1	96.2	171
1972–73	97.0	7.7	7.9	3.9	11.4	12.8	88.8	154
1973–74	104.7	8.4	8.0	5.2	11.4	11.8	96.8	165
1974–75	99.8	5.6	5.6	1.8	10.8	12.1	89.1	148
1975–76	121.0	9.4	7.8	-4.2	11.3	11.1	102.7	166
1976–77	111.2	12.7	11.4	1.9	9.2	9.3	99.2	159
1977–78	126.3	11.0	8.7	-1.1	10.0	9.1	108.8	173

Sources: Columns 1 and 4, from table 4-1; column 2, John Wall, "Foodgrain Management: Pricing, Procurement, Distribution, Import and Storage Policy," in *India: Occasional Papers*, World Bank Staff Working Paper 279 (World Bank, 1978), table 1, p. 88; columns 5 and 8, Government of India, Ministry of Agriculture and Irrigation, Directorate of Economics and Statistics, *Bulletin on Food Statistics, 1978*, 28th issue (Delhi: Controller of Publications, 1979), table 4, p. 38, table 11, p. 127, and preceding issues.

a. Data for calendar year following harvest year.
b. Column 1 + column 4, after deducting 12.5 percent of production for seed, feed, and waste.

surplus areas, it probably has the same effect as a tax on producers. In deficit areas, on the other hand, it should give an extra incentive to producers. The net disincentive effect will depend on the degree to which the system depresses the weighted average of procurement and open-market prices below the theoretical price that would prevail in an uncontrolled market. Unfortunately, the experience necessary for determining this theoretical price is lacking.

It is possible, however, to get a rough idea of year-to-year variations in the possible disincentive effects of the system by examining the average open-market, procurement, and weighted-average prices for India as a whole. These are shown separately for wheat and for rice in tables 4-3 and 4-4. For wheat, procurement prices were generally only moderately (10–20 percent) below the open market, but the margin has tended to be wider when food supplies were tight and it has narrowed in good years. The weighted-average price dropped from a peak in 1967–68 to remain steady from 1968–69 to 1973–74, but it rose sharply again in 1974–75 as a result of increases in procurement as well as open-market prices in that year. For rice, the margin has tended to be wider, rising from 25–30 percent to 50 percent in 1973–74 to 1975–76. Here again, the weighted-average price dropped from a peak in 1968–69, but started to rise again in 1971–72, mainly because of rising prices in the open market.

It should be noted that, in principle, the government procurement system can also serve as a price-support system in years of bumper crops. This seems to have occurred in some areas in 1975–76 and again in 1977–78, when the government stood ready to purchase, at the procurement price, any quantities offered to it.

Adequacy of Price Incentives

The adequacy of agricultural producers' returns is a controversial and elusive subject everywhere. It is rendered even more intractable by the prevalence of government intervention in agricultural markets. In India, low rice prices compared with world market prices, unfavorable product–fertilizer price ratios, and unfavorable developments in real prices have all been cited as evidence to support the thesis that producers' incentives have been insufficient.[8]

8. See, for example, Theodore W. Schultz, "Farm Entrepreneurs, Incentives, and Economic Policy," paper presented at Workshop on Resources, Incentives, and Agri-

Table 4-3. Open-Market and Government Procurement Prices of Wheat and Quantities Sold, India, 1966–67 to 1975–76

Marketing year (April–March)	Open market		Government procurement		Total		Government procurement price as percent of open-market price
	Price (rupees per quintal)[a]	Quantity (millions of metric tons)	Price (rupees per quintal)[b]	Quantity (millions of metric tons)	Price (rupees per quintal)[c]	Quantity (millions of metric tons)	
1966–67	82	1.86	60	0.20	80	2.06	73
1967–68	102	1.82	80	0.89	95	2.71	78
1968–69	85	2.91	76	2.30	81	5.21	89
1969–70	91	2.95	76	2.39	84	5.34	84
1970–71	85	2.80	76	3.19	80	5.99	89
1971–72	86	3.20	76	5.10	80	8.30	88
1972–73	93	3.24	76	5.00	83	8.24	82
1973–74	106	1.26	76	4.53	82	5.79	72
1974–75	159	3.25	105	1.95	139	5.20	66
1975–76	125	3.34	105	4.05	114	7.39	84

Source: Government of India, Ministry of Agriculture and Irrigation, Directorate of Economics and Statistics, *Bulletin on Food Statistics*, for years shown. Government procurement quantities from Wall, "Foodgrain Management," table 2, p. 90.
a. Average of selected markets.
b. Weighted average of state procurement prices.
c. Weighted average.

Table 4-4. Open-Market and Government Procurement Prices of Rice and Quantities Sold, India, 1967–68 to 1975–76

Marketing year (October–September)	Open market		Government procurement		Total		Government procurement price as percent of open-market price
	Price (rupees per quintal)[a]	Quantity (millions of metric tons)	Price (rupees per quintal)[b]	Quantity (millions of metric tons)	Price (rupees per quintal)[c]	Quantity (millions of metric tons)	
1967–68	124	4.42	85	3.23	107	7.65	69
1968–69	112	6.93	85	3.43	123	10.36	76
1969–70	118	6.54	85	2.94	108	9.48	72
1970–71	115	7.45	85	3.20	106	10.65	74
1971–72	126	7.19	85	3.12	114	10.31	67
1972–73	153	6.56	85	2.71	133	9.27	56
1973–74	214	5.99	110	3.51	173	9.50	51
1974–75	233	4.91	115	3.80	181	8.71	49
1975–76	220	6.25	115	6.32	167	12.57	52

Source: Same as table 4-3.
a. Average of selected markets.
b. Weighted average of state procurement prices.
c. Weighted average.

First we shall examine the absolute level of grain prices in India in relation to world prices and Indian production costs; second, the evolution, in real terms, of producer prices and gross returns; and third, the relationship between variations in real prices and variations in fertilizer use and weather-adjusted yields. The feasibility and probable effects of increased price supports or producers' subsidies are discussed in chapter 9.

Price Levels and Production Costs

The current wheat support (procurement) price in India is $130 per metric ton. This is slightly above the 1978 price received by American growers (which includes a subsidy of about $20) and slightly below the world market price. On the other hand, the support (procurement) price for rice is only $143 per ton (milled basis), less than half the world price.[9] These comparisons are misleading, however. The high world market price for rice is determined by the high supply price of American rice and Thai export taxes. As can be seen from tables 4-5 and 4-6, production costs of rice in India are only about 40 percent higher than those for wheat.

Do producer prices cover production costs? The available evidence suggests that they do, for both wheat and rice. Data for 1971–72 indicate that the wheat procurement price (76 rupees per quintal, or $102 per metric ton) was well above estimated production costs in three major wheat-producing states. If allowance is made for quantities sold in the open market, the average price received by Indian wheat growers (80 rupees per quintal or $107 per metric ton) exceeded production costs by about 50 percent and the then-prevailing world price ($73 per metric ton) by a similar percentage.[10]

For rice, the procurement price in 1971–72, 85 rupees per quintal or $113 per metric ton, although well below the world price of about $145

---

culture, University of Chicago, September 26–28, 1977; C. Peter Trimmer and Walter P. Falcon, "The Political Economy of Rice Production and Trade in Asia," in Lloyd G. Reynolds, ed., *Agriculture in Development Theory* (Yale University Press, 1975), pp. 373–408; Vasant A. Sukhatme, "The Utilization of High-Yielding Rice and Wheat Varieties in India: An Economic Assessment" (Ph.D. dissertation, University of Chicago, 1977).

9. *Foreign Agricultural Trade of the United States,* January 1979; world price for U.S. hard winter wheat (12 percent protein) c.i.f. Rotterdam; for rice, 5 percent broken, f.o.b. Bangkok.

10. Producer prices from table 4-3. Production costs from table 4-5. World price from *Foreign Agricultural Trade of the United States,* January 1973.

Table 4-5. *Cost of Production of Wheat in Three Major Wheat-Growing States, India, 1971–72*
Rupees per quintal

State	Cost[a]			
	A_1	A_2	B	C
Haryana	21.13	21.59	40.62	49.53
Punjab	29.02	31.37	53.22	59.71
Uttar Pradesh	21.11	21.53	43.40	50.38
Average	23.75	24.83	45.75	53.20

Source: Government of India, Ministry of Agriculture, Directorate of Economics and Statistics, "Report on Cost of Production of Wheat During the 1971–72 Crop Season for Haryana, Punjab and Uttar Pradesh," n.d.

  a. Definition of costs:

    A_1 = All paid-out costs or expenses incurred in cash and kind on material inputs, hired human labor, and bullock and machine labor.

    A_2 = Cost A_1 plus rent paid for leased-in land.

    B = Cost A_2 plus rental value of owned land and interest on owned fixed capital excluding land.

    C = Cost B plus imputed value of family labor.

Table 4-6. *Cost of Production of Rice in Five Major Rice-Growing States, India, 1971–72*
Rupees per quintal

State	Cost[a]			
	A_1	A_2	B	C
Andhra Pradesh	41.63	43.12	73.69	77.81
Tamil Nadu	45.83	50.34	77.31	80.74
Assam	21.92	24.58	60.50	75.35
West Bengal	24.04	25.15	61.21	81.77
Orissa	22.01	24.64	49.01	60.59
Average	31.08	33.57	64.34	75.25

Source: Government of India, Ministry of Agriculture and Irrigation, Directorate of Economics and Statistics, "Estimates of Cost of Production of Paddy," n.d.

  a. Costs are as defined in table 4-5.

per ton, was sufficient to cover production costs, broadly defined, in each of five major rice-producing states. Moreover, if allowance is made for the quantities sold in the open market, the average price received by Indian growers rises to 114 rupees per quintal, or $150 per metric ton—about equal to the world price and 50 percent above production costs.[11]

Comparable data for more recent years are available only for wheat in the Punjab (see table 4-7). The data suggest that the margin between the procurement price and the broadly defined cost of production nar-

    11. Producer prices from table 4-4. Production costs from table 4-6. World price (first grade f.o.b. Bangkok) from *Foreign Agricultural Trade of the United States,* January 1973.

Table 4-7. *Cost of Production of Wheat in Punjab, 1970–71 to 1974–75*
Rupees per quintal

Year	Cost[a]				Procurement price[b]	Average price[b]
	A_1	A_2	B	C		
1970–71	27.07	28.44	54.34	61.04	76	80
1971–72	29.02	31.37	53.22	59.71	76	80
1972–73	32.81	36.65	61.24	67.10	76	83
1973–74	36.88	41.08	67.33	74.34	76	82
1974–75	39.12	42.00	78.85	87.76	105	139

Sources: "Cost of Production of Wheat in Punjab," *Agricultural Situation in India* (September 1975), p. 443; "Cost of Production of Wheat in Punjab during 1974–75," *Agricultural Situation in India* (October 1976), p. 1.
a. Costs are as defined in table 4-5.
b. From table 4-3.

rowed until 1973–74, when it barely covered costs. The margin increased again in 1974–75, when procurement prices were raised by 38 percent. The margin between the average producer price and costs of production was wider throughout but also narrowed considerably between 1971–72 and 1973–74.

Evolution of Real Prices and Returns

It would seem reasonable to expect that variations in the degree of profitability of grain production, such as are suggested by table 4-7, would influence the use of inputs (primarily fertilizer) and, hence, grain yields. In the absence of reliable measurements of profitability, such indexes as grain–fertilizer price ratios, real grain prices (that is, the ratio of the index of grain prices to the general wholesale price index), or real gross returns per hectare must be used. The farmer's response may be represented by variations in fertilizer use per hectare and by weather-adjusted yields. These indexes are shown, separately for wheat and rice, in figures 4-1 and 4-2.

The best of the three indexes of profitability is, without doubt, the index of real gross returns per hectare, because it takes account of the effects of increasing productivity. Measured by this index, the profitability of wheat production rose steadily in the 1960s, a rise which was accompanied by rapid increases in fertilizer use and yields. The real price of wheat and the wheat–fertilizer price ratio began to decline in 1967–68, but this had no discernible effect on fertilizer use and yields because total returns continued to rise.

After 1971–72, the economic factors became less favorable to the wheat grower as both real prices and productivity stagnated. Prices and

Figure 4-1. *Indexes of Profitability, Fertilizer Consumption, and Weather-Adjusted Yields, Wheat, India, 1961–62 to 1977–78*

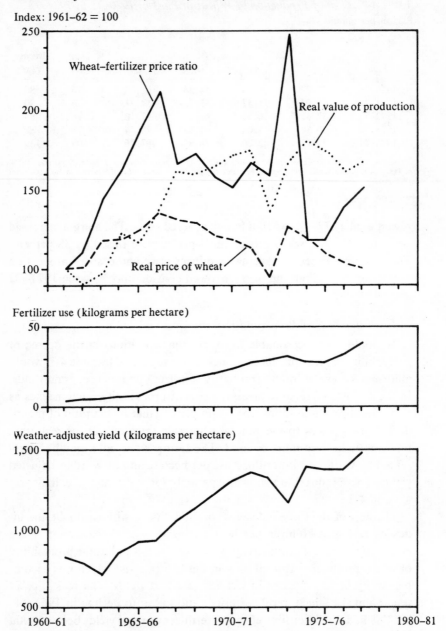

Index: 1961–62 = 100

Wheat–fertilizer price ratio

Real value of production

Real price of wheat

Fertilizer use (kilograms per hectare)

Weather-adjusted yield (kilograms per hectare)

Source: Price data, Government of India, Ministry of Agriculture and Irrigation, Directorate of Economics and Statistics, *Bulletin of Food Statistics*, various issues. Weather-adjusted yields and fertilizer consumption, table 3-3.

Figure 4-2. *Indexes of Profitability, Fertilizer Consumption, and Weather-Adjusted Yields, Rice, India, 1961–62 to 1977–78*

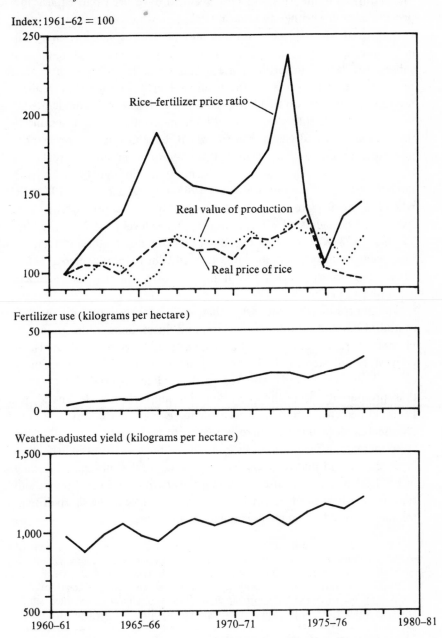

Index: 1961–62 = 100

Rice–fertilizer price ratio

Real value of production

Real price of rice

Fertilizer use (kilograms per hectare)

Weather-adjusted yield (kilograms per hectare)

Source: Price data, same as figure 4-1. Weather-adjusted yields and fertilizer consumption, table 3-6.

total returns for the 1972–73 crop seem to have been particularly low because of poor weather and soaring inflation, which were not fully offset by improved wheat prices, and this may help to explain the sharp dip in weather-adjusted yields in the following year. The leveling-off and subsequent decline in fertilizer use beginning in 1973–74 is, of course, related to the energy crisis and the upsurge of fertilizer prices; but fertilizer use resumed its upward trend in 1976–77 as fertilizer prices moderated.[12]

For rice, there is less variation in both the profitability indexes and in the weather-adjusted yields than for wheat, but this does not necessarily indicate a cause-and-effect relation. Profitability as measured by real gross returns per hectare showed a slowly rising trend through 1973–74, with the exception of the poor crop years 1965–66, 1966–67, and 1972–73, when low yields were only partly offset by higher rice prices. The sharp rise in weather-adjusted yields to a new, higher level in 1975–76, 1976–77, and 1977–78 cannot be explained by economic factors; in fact, the improvement (which undoubtedly was partly due to sharply increased fertilizer use) occurred despite declining real prices of rice and mediocre gross returns per hectare.

The impression that emerges is that, with few exceptions, fluctuations in real prices and returns per hectare, and fluctuations in the grain–fertilizer price ratios, did not exert a significant influence on fertilizer use or on weather-adjusted yields. Technological factors, notably the availability of fertilizer, water, and improved seeds, and managerial skills, rather than profitability, were the overriding limiting factors.[13] In general, returns per hectare seem to have been adequate to achieve otherwise attainable increases in inputs. There is reason to believe, however, that the steep increase in fertilizer prices in 1974 did have a depressing effect on fertilizer use and that recovery was facilitated by the subsequent decline in fertilizer prices. It is also likely that the sharp drop in real prices and returns for wheat produced in 1972–73 played a role in the sharp drop in weather-adjusted wheat yields in the following year.

12. The sharp upsurge of the wheat–fertilizer price ratio in 1973–74 was the result of a sharp upward adjustment of procurement prices not accompanied by increased fertilizer prices (which doubled in the following crop year).

13. Dharm Narain came to similar conclusions in his study, "Growth of Productivity in Indian Agriculture," *Indian Journal of Agricultural Economics,* vol. 32 (January–March 1977), pp. 1–44. With regard to fertilizer use, he finds that "technological progress has exerted a far greater influence . . . than the price of fertilizer relative to the prices of agricultural commodities" (p. 29).

CHAPTER FIVE

Institutional Factors

IN ALL developing countries, the agrarian structure is a passionately de-bated issue in which social, political, and economic considerations are frequently intermingled. It is therefore pertinent to emphasize at the out-set that it is not the purpose of this study to evaluate the existing rural institutions in India from the point of view of income distribution, social equity, or social and political stability. Rather, our objective is to examine the effects of land distribution, the credit structure, and land tenure on food production, on the rate of adoption of new technology, and on the marketable surplus.[1]

Land Distribution

Farms in India are small by American or even European standards: the average size of the operating unit is 2.3 hectares. Fifty-one percent of the farms operate less than 1 hectare; 70 percent less than 2 hectares. These small farms, however, account for only 21 percent of the total culti-vated area. At the other end of the scale, 15 percent of the farms cultivate

1. Readers interested in the effects of the green revolution on income distribution and the rural social structure will find an abundant literature ranging from more or less severe critics like Francine R. Frankel (*India's Green Revolution: Economic Gains and Political Costs* [Princeton University Press, 1971]), Keith Griffin (*The Political Economy of Agrarian Change: An Essay on the Green Revolution* [Harvard University Press, 1974]), and Wolf Ladejinsky (*Agrarian Reform as Unfinished Business*, Louis J. Walinsky, ed. [Oxford University Press for the World Bank, 1977]), to more balanced appraisals by Bandhudas Sen (*The Green Revolution in India: A Perspective* [Wiley, 1974], and John W. Mellor (*The New Economics of Growth: A Strategy for India and the Developing World* [Cornell University Press, 1976], chap. 4).

more than 4 hectares but they account for over 60 percent of the total cultivated area. Only 4 percent of all farms cultivate more than 10 hectares; these "large" farms account for 31 percent of the cultivated land.[2]

Table 5-1. *Farms, by Size of Operating Unit, India, 1970–71*

Size of operating unit (hectares)	Number (millions)	Cultivated area (millions of hectares)	Percent of all farms	Percent of total cultivated area
Less than 1	35.7	14.5	50.6	9.0
1–2	13.4	19.3	19.0	11.9
2–4	10.7	30.0	15.2	18.5
4–10	7.9	48.2	11.3	29.7
Over 10	2.8	50.1	3.9	30.9
All	70.5	162.12	100.0	100.0

Source: Government of India, Ministry of Agriculture and Irrigation, Department of Agriculture, *All India Report on Agricultural Census, 1970–71* (Delhi: Controller of Publications, 1975), table 8.2, p. 26.

The inequality of land distribution is mitigated by the better quality of land in small farms. The proportion of land under irrigation on farms of less than 1 hectare is 34 percent; on farms of 1–2 hectares, 28 percent; on farms of over 10 hectares, only 13 percent.[3]

The pattern of land ownership (see table 5-2) is similar to that of the operating units.[4] Small holdings predominate: 78 percent of the holdings measure less than 2 hectares (5 acres), but they account for 24.5 percent of the total area.[5] Only 5.4 percent of the holdings are over 6 hectares (15 acres), but they account for 39.4 percent of the total area.[6]

The pattern of land ownership has not changed much over the past

2. Data for 1970–71. See table 5-1.

3. Government of India, Ministry of Agriculture and Irrigation, Department of Agriculture, *All India Report on Agricultural Census, 1970–71* (Delhi: Controller of Publications, 1975), pp. 26–27. See also C. H. Hanumantha Rao, *Agricultural Production Functions, Costs and Returns in India,* Institute of Economic Growth (Delhi), Studies in Economic Growth, no. 5 (Bombay: Asia Publishing House, 1965); and B. Sen, "Opportunities in the Green Revolution," *Economic and Political Weekly,* Review of Agriculture, March 28, 1970, pp. A-33–A-40.

4. These data on land ownership, from the 26th round of the *National Sample Survey,* are not strictly comparable with those of the Agricultural Census on operating units because of differences in concepts, methodology, and coverage.

5. It can be seen that over half of these holdings—36 million—are holdings of less than 1 acre, and average only 0.14 acre.

6. Differences in the profiles of the two distributions reflect the tendency of large farms to rent additional land from small and medium-size landholders.

Table 5-2. Land Ownership, by Size of Holding, India, 1953–54, 1961–62, and 1971–72

Size of holding (acres)	1953–54						1961–62						1971–72					
	Number of households		Acres held				Number of households		Acres held				Number of households		Acres held			
	Millions	Per cent of total	Millions	Per cent of total	Average size (acres)		Millions	Per cent of total	Millions	Per cent of total	Average size (acres)		Millions	Per cent of total	Millions	Per cent of total	Average size (acres)	
Under 1	15.4	31.5	4.2	1.4	0.3		23.6	36.9	5.1	1.6	0.2		35.6	44.0	4.9	1.6	0.1	
1–5	17.4	35.6	45.7	15.0	2.6		22.5	35.2	58.5	18.4	2.6		27.4	33.8	71.2	22.9	2.6	
5–15	11.1	22.7	95.2	31.2	8.5		13.0	20.3	109.7	34.5	8.4		13.6	16.7	112.5	36.1	8.3	
15–50	4.3	8.8	106.8	35.0	24.8		4.5	7.0	109.3	34.4	24.2		4.1	5.0	96.9	31.1	23.9	
Over 50	0.6	1.2	53.6	17.6	88.7		0.4	0.6	35.4	11.1	81.0		0.4	0.4	25.9	8.3	73.9	
All	48.9	100.0	305.4	100.0	6.2		64.0	100.0	317.9	100.0	5.0		81.0	100.0	311.2	100.0	3.8	

Source: For 1971–72, Government of India, Ministry of Planning, Department of Statistics, National Sample Survey Organization, *National Sample Survey*, 26th Round: July 1971–September 1972, *Tables on Land Holdings, All India*, no. 215 (NSSO, 1976), table 1, p. 13, and previous issues for years shown. Figures are rounded.

few decades. Such changes as have occurred were in the direction of a wider spread of land ownership and a decline in the number and size of large holdings. The number of households owning land increased from 49 million in 1953–54 to 81 million in 1971–72. The largest increase occurred in the smallest size group (less than 1 acre) but without a significant increase in the total area occupied by these holdings. Small holdings from 1 to 5 acres increased significantly in numbers as well as total area owned. Medium-size holdings (5 to 15 acres) also increased in numbers and area, though to a lesser extent. Large holdings (15 to 50 acres) increased in numbers and total area until 1961–62 but declined in the following decade. Very large holdings declined sharply in numbers and total area owned. The average size of holdings remained fairly stable except in the two extreme size groups (less than 1 acre and over 50 acres).

Attempts to interpret this evolution and to isolate the factors contributing to it are hampered by a lack of reliable data.[7] The increase in the number of very small holdings and their declining size may reflect demographic pressure and impoverishment, but it could also mean that previously landless households have been able to purchase small parcels of land. Ceilings on land ownership and land transfers in anticipation of ceilings undoubtedly played a role in the decline of large holdings.[8] Small farmers, once frequently forced to sell out to moneylenders, are now assisted by the state. And while there were many cases of eviction of tenants, there also were instances of acquisition of land by tenants, with the help of favorable legislation.

Farm Size and Productivity

The relation between farm size and productivity has been studied extensively in India. Two main issues have emerged. It is often suggested that a redistribution of land would increase food production because small farms are more productive. On the other hand, it appears that the

7. See V. S. Vyas, "Some Aspects of Structural Change in Indian Agriculture," *Indian Journal of Agricultural Economics,* vol. 34 (January–March 1979), pp. 1–18.

8. There are indications that in many cases these transfers were pro forma to other members of the family, who would then lease the land back to the former owner. See Ladejinsky, *Agrarian Reform as Unfinished Business,* pp. 511–13, 540–41.

yield gap between large and small farmers is narrowing, since the latter find it more difficult to adopt new technology.

What is the evidence on these two points? That small farms are more productive per unit of land than large farms is well established. Farm management studies conducted in the fifties and sixties show an inverse relationship between farm size and value of production per acre owned. A consistent pattern was observed in all states.[9] More recent data show that the inverse relationship between size and productivity still holds. Thus sample data for the Punjab for 1971–72[10] show an inverse relationship between farm size and production per net cropped hectare on both tractorized and nontractorized farms (see table 5-3). The same inverse relationship emerges from the stratified all-India sample of 1,444 farms collected by the National Council of Applied Economic Research (NCAER) in 1970–71 (see table 5-4).

Is the higher yield per hectare of small farms due to higher labor intensity or could it be due to extraneous factors such as higher land quality? The main index of land quality in India is whether or not the land can be irrigated, as well as the adequacy and dependability of irrigation.

The NCAER data show that small farms tend to have a higher ratio of irrigated land than larger farms (see table 5-5). No doubt this explains in part why smaller farms are more productive, but it cannot account for all of the difference. In fact, in the Punjab sample (table 5-3), nontractorized farms have the same percent of irrigated land regardless of size. In this case, the higher productivity of small farms can be traced very clearly to their greater use of double cropping. Higher cropping intensity also seems to be an independent factor in the NCAER sample, even allowing for the fact that irrigation is generally a prerequisite for double cropping. For example, farms of less than 2 hectares show a distinctly higher cropping intensity than those between 2 and 6 hectares, although the percent of

9. For a summary see Jagdish N. Bhagwati and Sukhamoy Chakravarty, "Contributions to Indian Economic Analysis: A Survey," *American Economic Review,* vol. 59 (September 1969), pt. 2: Supplement, pp. 1–73. See also Manabendu Chattopadhyay and Ashok Rudra, "Size-Productivity Revisited," *Economic and Political Weekly,* Review of Agriculture, September 25, 1976, pp. A-104–A-116.

10. Shyamal Roy, "Effects of Farm Tractorization on Productivity and Labor Employment on Punjab Farms, India" (Ph.D. dissertation, University of Missouri–Columbia, 1974). See also Shyamal Roy and Melvin G. Blase, "Farm Tractorization, Productivity and Labor Employment: A Case Study of Indian Punjab," *Journal of Development Studies,* vol. 14 (January 1978), pp. 193–209.

Table 5-3. *Farm Size and Value of Production[a] per Net Cropped Hectare, Punjab, 1971–72*

Farm size (hectares)	Tractorized farms				Nontractorized farms			
	Production per hectare (rupees)	Cropping intensity index[b]	Percent of cropped area irrigated	Percent of cropped area under HYVs	Production per hectare (rupees)	Cropping intensity index[b]	Percent of cropped area irrigated	Percent of cropped area under HYVs
Under 6	3,551	195	90	51	2,950	165	89	39
6–12	2,980	167	85	51	2,548	150	88	39
Over 12	2,597	153	91	41	2,160	131	89	37
All farms	3,109	174	88	47	2,753	157	89	38

Source: Shyamal Roy, "Effects of Farm Tractorization on Productivity and Labor Employment on Punjab Farms, India" (Ph.D. dissertation, University of Missouri–Columbia. 1974), pp. 24–25, 45.
a. Includes all crops.
b. The ratio of gross cropped area to net cropped area, times 100.

Table 5-4. *Value of Production,*[a] *by Farm Size, All India, 1968–71*
Rupees per hectare

Farm size (hectares)	1968–69	1969–70	1970–71	Percent increase, 1968–69 to 1970–71
Under 2	1,890	1,957	2,026	7
2–6	1,475	1,554	1,651	12
6–10	1,139	1,109	1,253	10
Over 10	690	786	924	34
All farms	1,473	1,532	1,638	11

Source: Unpublished data provided by National Council of Applied Economic Research, New Delhi.
a. Includes all crops.

Table 5-5. *Cropping Intensity and Percent of Cultivated Area Irrigated, by Farm Size, India, 1970–71*

Farm size (hectares)	Cropping intensity index	Percent of area irrigated
Under 2	151	50
2–6	139	51
6–10	128	38
Over 10	121	29
All farms	139	46

Source: Unpublished data provided by National Council of Applied Economic Research, New Delhi.

irrigated land is virtually the same in the two size groups (table 5-5). A multiple regression analysis by Surjit Bhalla[11] shows that the inverse relationship between farm size and value of output per hectare holds even after differences in land value are taken into account.

It is interesting to note that the higher productivity per hectare of small farms is not due to greater use of fertilizer; in fact, fertilizer use tends to be greater on medium and large farms (table 5-6). This suggests that small farms could increase their advantage over larger farms, in terms of productivity per hectare, if existing impediments to fertilizer consumption could be removed.

11. Surjit S. Bhalla, "Farm Size, Productivity and Technical Change in Indian Agriculture," in R. Albert Berry and William R. Cline, *Agrarian Structure and Productivity in Developing Countries* (Johns Hopkins University Press, 1979), app. A, pp. 141–93.

Table 5-6. *Fertilizer Consumption, by Farm Size, India, 1968–69 to 1970–71*

Kilograms NPK per net cropped hectare

Crop and year	Farm size (hectares)			
	Under 2.5	2.5–8.5	Over 8.5	All farms
Rice				
1968–69	15.33	20.05	15.97	17.57
1969–70	12.74	18.11	25.17	16.40
1970–71	21.51	20.77	45.62	23.33
Wheat				
1968–69	16.32	27.31	28.65	25.25
1969–70	20.36	37.79	20.55	30.19
1970–71	23.13	31.47	28.20	28.08

Source: National Council of Applied Economic Research, *Fertilizer Use on Selected Crops in India* (New Delhi: NCAER and the Fertilizer Association of India, 1974), table 3, p. T-4; table 24, p. T-25.

The available evidence thus supports the thesis that small farms are more productive per unit of land.[12] It does not necessarily follow that small farms are superior in productivity per person employed, or—what is more relevant—in overall productivity per unit of all inputs combined. But given the relative scarcity of land and capital and the abundance of cheap and underemployed labor (and the lack of alternative employment opportunities), there is unquestionably a strong case for maximizing output per hectare at this point.[13]

On the second point at issue, the evidence does suggest a narrowing of the yield gap between large and small farms as a result of the green revolution. Thus, Lockwood, Mukherjee, and Shand[14] found that in the wheat-growing regions, large farmers were quicker to adopt HYVs. For example, 90 percent in the top size decile, but only 45 percent in the lowest decile, used high-yielding seeds in 1969–70. Similar results were found in the rice-growing regions.

12. However, factors other than farm size (fertilizer use or percent of land irrigated) can be shown to be more important determinants of productivity per hectare than farm size. See Vyas, "Some Aspects of Structural Change."

13. See Peter Dorner and Don Kanel, "The Economic Case for Land Reform," U.S. Agency for International Development, paper prepared for Spring Review of Land Reform, June 1970, SR/LR/A-3.

14. Brian Lockwood, P. K. Mukherjee, and R. T. Shand, *The High Yielding Varieties Program in India*, pt. 1 (Government of India, Program Evaluation Organization, and Canberra: Department of Economics, Research School of Pacific Studies, Australian National University, 1971), pp. 88–93.

More detailed evidence is provided by the NCAER sample survey, taken on the same farms for three consecutive years, 1968–69, 1969–70, and 1970–71. The trend of production values per hectare during this period shows that small farms *have* participated in the green revolution, but the gains were not quite as great as on medium-size farms and substantially less than in the largest size group (see table 5-4). Larger farms were quicker to adopt the HYVs (table 5-7) and, more significantly, showed greater gains in the percent of the area sown to HYVs (table 5-8).

Table 5-7. *Percent of Farmers Using HYVs, by Farm Size, India, 1968–69 to 1970–71*

Farm size (hectares)	1968–69	1969–70	1970–71	Percent gain, 1968–69 to 1970–71
Under 2	26	27	37	42
2–6	30	35	38	27
6–10	31	43	47	52
Over 10	34	36	40	18
All farms	29	34	39	34

Source: Unpublished data provided by National Council of Applied Economic Research, New Delhi.

Table 5-8. *Percent of Sown Area under HYVs, by Farm Size, India, 1968–69 to 1970–71*

Farm size (hectares)	1968–69	1969–70	1970–71	Percent gain, 1968–69 to 1970–71
Under 2	15.8	11.3	18.5	17
2–6	13.1	11.4	15.8	21
6–10	13.5	12.9	17.7	31
Over 10	10.5	9.4	17.0	62
All farms	13.7	11.5	17.1	25

Source: Unpublished data provided by National Council of Applied Economic Research, New Delhi.

Other studies tend to corroborate these findings. Thus, Bhattacharya and Saini found a weakening of the relationship between size and value of output per acre over time in Muzaffarnagar (Uttar Pradesh) and Ferozepore (Punjab).[15] Chadha found that, for Punjab as a whole, "the

15. N. Bhattacharya and G. R. Saini, "Farm Size and Productivity: A Fresh Look," *Economic and Political Weekly,* Review of Agriculture, June 24, 1972, pp. A-63–A-72; and G. R. Saini, "Green Revolution and the Distribution of Farm Incomes," ibid., March 27, 1976, pp. A-17–A-22.

relationship between farm size and productivity [expressed in value of output per acre] is tending to disappear." However, this is true "more surely in areas in which the increase in capital:labor ratio on large farms has taken place rather pronouncedly. . . . In areas where capital expansion in relation to labor input is yet at comparatively low levels, the inverse relationship still holds."[16] In regions that are in the intermediate range of the capital–labor ratio, there is a tendency for the farm size-productivity relationship to catch up with the more capital-intensive areas.

Credit

Fertilizer use may be expected to depend on the availability of credit and on the farmer's willingness to incur the risks involved in using credit. Indeed, it is often charged that small farmers have inadequate access to credit, particularly low-cost credit provided by official credit institutions. Others contend that small farmers are reluctant to use credit even when it is available because of the problem of repayment in the event of crop failure.

As can be seen from table 5-9, the small farmer tends to borrow about as much as or more than farmers with larger holdings (thus casting doubt on his supposed reluctance to use credit). But the smallest size group seems to have greater difficulty in obtaining credit from credit institutions than do medium and large farmers. Institutional credit is available at significantly lower interest rates than credit from moneylenders, on whom small farmers depend for two-thirds and medium farmers for well over half their credit needs. Large farmers, by contrast, obtain one-third of their credit from institutions and almost half from friends and relatives, on what are presumed to be very easy terms (table 5-10).

Although the evidence is not conclusive, it does suggest that small farmers might borrow more if institutional credit were more readily available to them. As it is, the amounts borrowed for current farming expenses seem barely sufficient to pay for the modest quantities of fertilizer used. Given more liberal credit, fertilizer use per hectare on small farms might rise to levels equal to or exceeding those on large farms.

16. G. K. Chadha, "Farm Size and Productivity Revisited: Some Notes from Recent Experience of Punjab," *Economic and Political Weekly,* Review of Agriculture, September 30, 1978, p. A-95.

Table 5-9. *Rural Credit, by Farm Size, India, 1970–71*

| Size of holding (hectares) | Percent of borrowing households | Amount borrowed per hectare (rupees) | | | Percent borrowed from institu- tional sources |
		Current farming expenses	Capital farming expenses	Total (current and capital)	
0–2	39.2	38	101	139	21.4
2–4	47.2	44	83	127	34.8
4–6	44.8	36	102	138	37.4
6 and above	39.5	22	69	91	32.3
All holdings	41.6	33	83	116	30.3

Source: National Council of Applied Economic Research, *Credit Requirements for Agriculture* (New Delhi: NCAER, 1974), table 9, p. 59; table 13, pp. 62–63; table 16, pp. 66–67; table 35, pp. 82–83.

Table 5-10. *Percent of Agricultural Credit Received from Various Sources and Average Interest Rates, by Farm Size, India, 1970–71*[a]

| Source | Size of holding (hectares) | | | | |
	Under 2	2–4	4–6	6 and above	All farms
Government	3.2	5.3	4.1	2.4	3.6
	(8.9)	(9.0)	(8.3)	(8.4)	(8.8)
Cooperatives	16.7	25.5	24.8	25.4	22.7
	(8.9)	(9.1)	(9.0)	(9.0)	(9.0)
Commercial banks	1.5	4.0	8.5	4.5	4.0
	(7.2)	(8.1)	(9.4)	(9.2)	(8.4)
Moneylenders	66.2	59.6	54.9	23.6	49.6
	(22.5)	(20.9)	(23.3)	(16.3)	(21.8)
Friends and relatives	11.0	5.1	2.5	44.0	18.8
	(0.0)	(0.0)	(0.0)	(0.0)	(0.0)
All sources	100.0	100.0	100.0	100.0	100.0
	(16.0)	(14.3)	(14.9)	(9.0)	(14.8)

Source: National Council of Applied Economic Research, *Credit Requirements for Agriculture*, table 35, pp. 82–83; table 47, p. 95.

a. Figures in parentheses are average rates of interest.

Land Tenure

Quite apart from the size distribution of operating units, changes in land tenure may influence production. In general, a tenant or share-cropper, particularly where there is an absentee owner, is presumed to put in more effort (including that of his family) than hired laborers. Where a farm is operated by the owner and is not too large for him to supervise effectively, the disadvantage of the lower productivity of hired laborers may be offset by the advantages of more efficient and flexible management. While owners and tenants *can* cooperate effectively in arriving at management decisions, such cooperation comes under increasing strains in periods of rapid technological innovation.[17] Since tenants and sharecroppers operate under a perpetual threat of eviction, they will be reluctant to invest labor, let alone other resources, in permanent improvements.

Unfortunately, not enough data are available to test the validity of this argument. Rao suggests that sharecropping may be beneficial in areas of relative economic stability where there is little scope for decisionmaking and where the entrepreneurial profit is low. But sharecropping may cease to be beneficial as profitable modern inputs are introduced. Hence, Rao argues that changes in the lease agreements in favor of owner operation may be necessary when the introduction of profitable inputs raises the incentive for investment and widens the scope for decisionmaking.[18]

The introduction of modern inputs may explain the apparent trend during the past two decades from tenancy arrangements to direct operation by the owner. Dharm Narain and P. C. Joshi, on the basis of the National Sample Survey (NSS) data, found that the leased area, which constituted about a fifth of the operated area in 1953–54, dropped to one-eighth in 1960–61 and to a little more than one-tenth in 1961–62. In order to judge the reliability of the data, they investigated whether the results of the village surveys conducted at about the same time in various states in India corroborated the NSS findings. Their conclusion was "that the phenomenon of decline in the weight of tenancy, as reflected in the figures of leased-in area, is by and large real." Self-cultivation of land in these states was increasing and more land was being withdrawn from sharecroppers and tenants. An important reason for the decline in tenancy was described as "improved prospects for self-cultivation resulting partly from the rise in agricultural prices and partly from the provision of infrastructure supporting and promoting improved technology."[19]

Data on tenancy and sharecropping are not as extensive for more

17. Richard H. Day, "The Economics of Technological Change and the Demise of the Sharecropper," *American Economic Review,* vol. 57 (June 1967), pp. 427–49.

18. C. H. Hanumantha Rao, "Uncertainty, Enterpreneurship, and Sharecropping in India," *Journal of Political Economy,* vol. 79 (May–June 1971), pp. 578–95; and Rao, *Technological Change and Distribution of Gains in Indian Agriculture,* Institute of Economic Growth (Delhi: Macmillan Co. of India, Ltd., for IEG, 1975).

19. Dharm Narain and P. C. Joshi, "Magnitude of Agricultural Tenancy," *Economic and Political Weekly,* Review of Agriculture, September 27, 1969, pp. A-140–A-141.

recent years as for the early sixties. However, since the profitability of cultivation increased considerably with the introduction of high-yielding varieties, one would expect to see increased self-cultivation and decreased tenancy during the 1960s. This appears to have happened in the states (Punjab, Haryana, Kerala, Jammu and Kashmir, Tamil Nadu, Karnataka, Marahashtra, and Gujarat) where productivity growth has been most rapid.[20]

In the Punjab, the percentage of owner-operated farms rose from 66 in 1957 to 81 in 1969–70, while tenant holdings declined from 33 percent to 19 percent.[21] Wolf Ladejinsky, who studied the problems of tenancy in the context of the new technology, observed for the state of Bihar that "as ownership of improved land is coming to be prized very highly there is mounting determination among owners not to permit the tenants to share in the rights of the land they cultivate. Their preference is to be rid of them. . . . One of the consequences of the green revolution is the weakening still further of their [tenants' and sharecroppers'] already very tenuous hold on the land."[22] In a later article he went on to say, "Now that green revolution land is practically invaluable, the owners would like to get rid of tenants altogether and resume the land for self-cultivation."[23] Ashok Rudhra and Shiela Bhalla arrived at similar conclusions.[24]

Whether this development, taken by itself, has helped or hindered the increase in production per hectare is impossible to prove statistically. While the substitution of hired labor for sharecroppers may reduce the motivation of the labor force, this may be offset by increased motivation and efficiency on the management side. Similarly, while the enlargement of the operating unit may lead to less intensive cultivation, this may be

20. Pranab Bardhan, "Variations in Extent and Forms of Agricultural Tenancy—II: Analysis of Indian Data across Regions and Over Time," *Economic and Political Weekly,* September 18, 1976, p. 1543.

21. Figures cited in B. Dasgupta, "Agrarian Change and the New Technology in India," UN Research Institute for Social Development, Geneva, 1976.

22. Wolf Ladejinsky, "Green Revolution in Bihar: The Kosi Area: A Field Trip," *Economic and Political Weekly,* Review of Agriculture, September 27, 1969, p. A-160.

23. Wolf Ladejinsky, "How Green Is the Indian Green Revolution?" *Economic and Political Weekly,* Review of Agriculture, December 29, 1973, p. A-137.

24. Ashok Rudhra, A. Majid, and B. D. Talib, "Big Farmers of Punjab: Some Preliminary Findings of a Sample Survey," *Economic and Political Weekly,* Review of Agriculture, September 27, 1969, pp. A-143–A-146; Shiela Bhalla, "Changes in Acreage and Tenure Structure of Land Holdings in Haryana, 1962–1972," ibid., March 26, 1977, pp. A-2–A-15.

offset by more rapid adoption of new technology by the larger operating unit.

Fragmentation of Holdings

The growth of population and the unrestricted operation of the laws of succession and inheritance have led to the subdivision of agricultural land in India into smaller and smaller parcels. "Sub-division brings in its wake the problem of fragmentation. As the family holding is partitioned after the death of the owner, each heir tries to secure a portion of all the different kinds of land that were included in the family holding. As a result no one gets all his land in one compact bloc."[25] In these circumstances, irrigation becomes difficult, and undersized and scattered parcels have generally led to low productivity, waste, and debt.

Efforts have been made to promote the consolidation of holdings but, except in Himachal Pradesh, Punjab, and Haryana (and to some extent in Maharashtra and Uttar Pradesh), progress has been slow. The Fifth Plan document states that "no law for effecting consolidation of holdings has yet been passed in the Andhra area of Andhra Pradesh, Kerala and Tamil Nadu." The laws of Gujarat, Madhya Pradesh, and West Bengal provide for consolidation on a voluntary basis. The other states have passed the necessary legislation for compulsory consolidation.[26] By 1973–74, about 39.3 million hectares of land had been consolidated (table 5-11).

Fragmentation of holdings thus continues to be a major obstacle to productivity growth in many of the states in India. The high rate of agricultural growth witnessed in Punjab and Haryana was greatly facilitated by the successful completion of the consolidation program.

Pros and Cons of Land Redistribution

The land reform legislation passed in the 1950s and early 1960s imposed ceilings on individual landholdings. The ceiling laws differed considerably from state to state as to levels of ceilings, their applicability to

25. Dhires Bhattacharyya, *Understanding India's Economy: A Course of Analysis*, vol. 1 (Calcutta: Progressive Publishers, 1969), p. 85.

26. Government of India, Planning Commission, *Draft Fifth Five Year Plan, 1974–79*, vol. 2 (New Delhi: Controller of Publications, 1974), p. 43.

Table 5-11. *Consolidation of Holdings, Selected States, India, 1973–74*
Millions of hectares

State	Total culti-vable area	Consolidation completed	Percent of area consolidated
Andhra Pradesh	15.5	0.36	2.3
Assam	2.7	...	...
Bihar	11.5	0.30	2.6
Gujarat	11.1	1.21	10.9
Haryana, Punjab, and Himachal Pradesh	8.8	8.80	100.0
Jammu and Kashmir	1.0	0.02	2.0
Kerala	2.3	...	...
Karnataka	12.4	1.01	8.1
Maharashtra	20.8	9.77	47.0
Madhya Pradesh	22.1	3.55	16.1
Orissa	7.6	...	...
Rajasthan	25.0	1.73	6.9
Tamil Nadu	8.2	...	...
Uttar Pradesh	20.1	11.77	58.6
West Bengal	5.9	...	...
All India	176.6	39.33	22.3

Source: Government of India, Ministry of Agriculture and Irrigation, *Report of the National Commission on Agriculture, 1976*, pt. 15: *Agrarian Reforms* (Delhi: Controller of Publications, 1976), pp. 233–34.

individuals or families, and transfers, partitions, and exemptions. Ceilings have ranged from 6–15 hectares in Kerala to 9–136 hectares in Rajasthan.[27]

A new law was passed in 1972, based on the recommendations of the Central Land Reforms Committee. It fixed ceilings ranging from 4 to 7 hectares for perennially irrigated best land and from 4 to 22 hectares for good to poor land, with adjustments for large families. The new land ceiling scheme is to be applied retroactively from January 24, 1971, by all states enacting ceiling legislation.[28]

The implementation of the land redistribution laws has been slow. As of 1977 only 1.6 million hectares (1.1 percent of the total cultivated

27. Gene Wunderlich, *Land Reforms in India*, U.S. Agency for International Development, Spring Review of Land Reform, Country Papers, 2nd ed., vol. 1, SR/LR/C-20 (U.S. Department of State, USAID, 1970), p. 35. See also Wolf Ladejinsky, "Agrarian Reform in India, October 1965," in Ladejinsky, *Agrarian Reform as Unfinished Business*, pp. 369–404.

28. Wolf Ladejinsky, "New Ceiling Round and Implementation Prospects," *Economic and Political Weekly*, Review of Agriculture, September 30, 1972, pp. A-125–A-132.

area) had been declared surplus, and only 0.55 million hectares had been distributed.[29] The entire surplus would provide land for about 800,000 two-hectare farms. It may be assumed that very little of this land is irrigated. The distribution has been completed only in the state of Jammu and Kashmir, though significant progress has been made in the states of Gujarat, Maharashtra, Uttar Pradesh, and Andhra Pradesh.

As mentioned earlier, the *prima facie* economic case for a more radical program of land redistribution rests, in large part, on the higher levels of production per hectare achieved by intensively cultivated small farms. In most cases, however, substantial investments in irrigation facilities (plus credit for the purchase of fertilizer and HYV seeds) will be necessary to realize the potential of intensive cultivation. A case can be made that such investments would pay off in time in terms of increased production.

Splitting up the large landholdings would not be without costs, however. Although small farmers have readily adopted the HYVs and other aspects of the new technology, land redistribution would undoubtedly involve some waste of managerial skills and efficiency. The fact that the gains in productivity brought by the green revolution have been greater on medium and large farms than on small farms suggests that it may also result in a slower rate of growth once the immediate benefits of a more intensive mode of cultivation are realized.

It is often pointed out that land redistribution would help to improve the food supply of the rural poor. This would be partly the result of increased production but it would also be at the expense of deliveries to the cities. The marketable surplus of grains today is largely supplied by the larger farms. In years of below-average production, it is becoming increasingly difficult to mobilize surpluses in the agricultural areas to meet the requirements of the rapidly growing urban centers. Land redistribution could aggravate this problem.

Finally, it should be kept in mind that the strategy centered on the promotion of small-scale agriculture, though necessary for immediate and compelling economic, social, and political reasons, is essentially a holding operation. Its principal economic justification is that it provides employment for surplus labor that cannot be absorbed rapidly by other economic sectors. But it cannot indefinitely (indeed, so far as the landless

29. Government of India, Ministry of Agriculture and Irrigation, *Report 1977–78* (Delhi: Government of India Press, 1978), p. 85.

are concerned, even now) serve as a sufficient manpower sponge. In the long run, India's development will depend on providing off-farm employment for the mass of unemployed and underemployed. A stage will be reached when the urban sector will have absorbed the unemployed laborers who crowd the urban slums and when the general level of productivity begins to exceed that which can be achieved on a small holding.

Effects of Tractorization

The introduction of the high-yielding varieties, along with increased use of fertilizers, water, and pesticides, considerably enhanced the scope for double and multiple cropping. The new varieties also made it profitable to irrigate and to bring land formerly used for pasture under cereal cultivation. These factors, plus the increasing stress on economies of time, led to a substantial increase in the demand for energy on the farm. The tractor population in India doubled between 1956 and 1971. Punjab and Haryana took the lead, accounting for more than 42 percent; Uttar Pradesh about 20 percent; and Rajasthan, Tamil Nadu, Maharashtra, and Gujarat, 6 to 8 percent each.

The increased use of tractors led to a controversy as to the desirability of a capital-intensive technology in a predominantly labor-abundant country. Some argued that farm tractorization induced a net additional demand for labor through changes in cropping intensity and crop rotations. Others feared that tractors would cause a considerable net displacement of labor.

From the point of view of a rational producer, investment in tractors is indicated when either the technical conditions of production are such that using tractors will cause an upward shift in the production function or the relative prices of labor and capital have shifted in favor of capital, or both. Considerations of technical efficiency have justified the use of tractors in some areas, as, for example, on certain types of soil in Rajasthan where bullock and human power is judged insufficient to clear, level, and plough land properly. The larger size of holdings, the high proportion of land under irrigation, and the widespread use of high-yielding varieties have created favorable conditions for the introduction of tractors for intensive cultivation in Western Uttar Pradesh, Punjab, and Haryana. A sharp increase in wages relative to the price of capital in the northern states, reflecting an acute shortage of labor during the peak agricultural season, also contributed to the use of tractors in these states. But since these favorable conditions do not exist in other states, tractorization in India has been largely confined to only a few states.

While the use of tractors can be justified on grounds of private profitability, the critical issue in a labor-surplus country is: do the economic advantages of farm tractorization offset the possible social costs of rural unemployment? The impact of tractorization on employment is the result of two opposite forces, one tending to displace labor immediately (as will be the case with the introduction of any kind of machinery) and the other tending to promote overall use of labor through increased cropping intensities, higher yields per acre, land reclamation programs, increased rural nonfarm employment, and so forth. The overall increase or decrease in the employment of labor depends on the relative strength of the two contending forces. Most of the studies conducted on the employment effects of farm tractorization are confined to those on the farm itself; they show that more jobs are created than displaced as new employment is generated for interculturing, harvesting, and similar activities. Acharya's study of Rajasthan for 1971–72, for instance, shows a 12.7 percent increase in employment on tractorized farms;[30] Rao notes a similar trend in Punjab in 1968–69.[31] Though Roy's study of Punjab in 1971–72 shows no statistically significant difference in total labor use per acre between tractorized and nontractorized farms, the employment of hired labor (casual and annual) on tractorized farms was twice that on farms without tractors.[32]

Tractorization was also found to have favorable effects on output per hectare. By speeding up operations, tractors facilitate the planting of more than one crop during the year. In the Punjab, this was reflected in the higher cropping intensity on tractorized farms (174 as compared with 157 on other farms). This relationship holds for small and large farms alike (see table 5-3). Other studies support this conclusion: a review of the literature indicates that the gross value of output per operated or net cropped area was greater on tractorized farms by more than 10 percent in 75 percent of the cases, and by more than 30 percent in one-third of

30. S. S. Acharya, "Green Revolution and Farm Employment," *Indian Journal of Agricultural Economics,* vol. 28 (July–September 1973), pp. 30–45.

31. C. H. Hanumantha Rao, "Employment Implications of the Green Revolution and Mechanization: A Case Study of the Punjab," in Nurul Islam, ed., *Agricultural Policy in Developing Countries* (Wiley, 1974), pp. 340–62.

32. Roy, "Effects of Farm Tractorization."

the cases reported.[33] Of course, increased productivity cannot be attributed to tractors alone. Production-function analysis suggests that tractors play a complementary or enabling role in the production process, raising the marginal productivity of other inputs.[34]

Tractorization is thus economically justified in the particular circumstances where it contributes significantly to multiple and intensive cropping and, thereby, to increased employment. However, if farm mechanization overtakes the pace of crop intensification, the effects on production per hectare and on employment could be adverse. The role of public policy is thus to ensure that farm mechanization is selective.

Research and Extension

Among developing countries, India is fortunate in having one of the more advanced agricultural education systems. Expenditures for agricultural research and education have been increased significantly during the past decade, from $180 million in the Fourth Plan to $262 million in the Fifth Plan and $531 million in the (new) Sixth Plan. The principal agencies through which agricultural research is conducted are the Indian Council of Agricultural Research, with its thirty central research institutes, twenty-one agricultural universities, and fifty-two all-India coordinated research projects.

The greatest need at this stage is for more effective ways of making the new technology available to individual farmers. Small farmers, in particular, need practical guidance in applying the technology best suited to their circumstances. India's agricultural extension service is spread very thinly—one village-level worker for about 1,000 to 1,200 farm families—less than one-third of the required ratio of one full-time worker for about 300 farm families.[35]

There have also been problems with the quality of the extension service. In the past, extension workers were expected to have received adequate training before they were hired, but no follow-up training was

33. Hans P. Binswanger, *The Economics of Tractors in the Indian Subcontinent: An Analytical Review* (Hyderabad, India: International Crops Research Institute for the Semi-Arid Tropics, 1977), p. 10.

34. Rao, "Employment Implications of the Green Revolution."

35. See *Report of the National Commission on Agriculture, 1976*, pt. 14: *Planning, Statistics and Administration,* Government of India, Ministry of Agriculture and Irrigation (Delhi: Controller of Publications, 1976).

required. The results have been disappointing. There was little give-and-take between farmers and extension agents; the extension program has "proved woefully short on how to demonstrate [the] use [of the new inputs] to the farmers in a practical way."[36]

Recently a new approach has been introduced, the "training and visit system."[37] Under this method, extension workers first acquaint themselves with the problems faced by farmers through visits to the farms. They then are trained by scientists on specific farm operations for each crop in each area one or two weeks before going out to advise farmers. The farmers are advised in small groups on each day in a different village on those operations. Thus, a prompt two-way communication is established between the farmer and the scientist on problems encountered by the farmer, through the medium of extension workers. The method was first tried in the Chambal area of Rajasthan with very good results. It has subsequently been extended to other areas of Rajasthan, West Bengal, Assam, Orissa, Bihar, Madhya Pradesh, and irrigated areas of Andhra Pradesh. About 13 percent of the farms are now covered by these projects; when fully developed, this ratio is scheduled to rise to 31 percent.

36. Ladejinsky, *Agrarian Reform as Unfinished Business,* pp. 407–13.
37. Daniel Benor and James Q. Harrison, *Agricultural Extension: The Training and Visit System* (World Bank, 1977).

CHAPTER SIX

Food Supplies and
Food Consumption

ALTHOUGH foodgrain production has increased about 50 percent since the early 1960s, this gain was largely offset by the growth of population in the last seventeen years (table 6-1, columns 1 and 5). Grain imports averaging 4.8 million tons (column 2) contributed about 5 percent of the total supply of foodgrains. Per capita net availability (column 6) in 1977–78 (172.5 kilograms) was about the same as in 1960–61.[1]

Foodgrain production varies considerably from year to year, with peaks and troughs deviating by as much as 14 million tons from the trend. The government has aimed at, but not quite succeeded in, stabilizing foodgrain supplies by imports and stock management: per capita food supplies dropped sharply in the two disaster years, 1965–66 and 1966–67, and also in 1972–73 and 1974–75 (column 6).

1. According to the National Commission on Agriculture, the failure of per capita foodgrain consumption to increase in the 1960s is consistent with what could be expected from the development of real incomes and of real prices of foodgrains: the effect of a 12.4 percent increase in real income per capita was almost exactly offset by the effect of a 14 percent increase in the real price of foodgrains.

The decline in per capita availability in 1972–76 is puzzling, since it occurred despite a slight increase in per capita real income and a decline in real prices of foodgrains. Changes in income distribution during this period or in the rate of urbanization also fail to explain this decline. A possible explanation is the failure of the availability statistics to reflect consumption generated by the release of private stocks. See J. S. Sarma and Shyamal Roy, "Behavior of Foodgrains Production and Consumption in India, 1960–1977," World Bank Staff Working Paper 339 (World Bank, 1979); and J. S. Sarma, "India—A Drive Towards Self-Sufficiency in Food Grains," *American Journal of Agricultural Economics,* vol. 60 (December 1978), pp. 859–64.

Table 6-1. *Foodgrain Production, Net Imports, Changes in Stocks, and Net Availability, India, 1960–61 to 1977–78*

Year	Net production (millions of tons)[a] (1)	Net imports (millions of tons)[b] (2)	Releases from government stocks (millions of tons)[c] (3)	Net availability (millions of tons) (4)	Population (millions) (5)	Per capita net availability (kilograms per year) (6)
1960–61	72.04	3.49	0.17	75.69	442.4	171.1
1961–62	72.08	3.63	0.36	76.08	452.2	168.2
1962–63	70.29	4.54	0.02	74.85	462.0	162.0
1963–64	70.61	6.25	1.24	78.11	472.1	165.5
1964–65	78.20	7.44	−1.06	84.57	482.5	175.3
1965–66	63.30	10.31	−0.14	73.48	493.2	149.0
1966–67	64.95	8.66	0.26	73.87	504.2	146.5
1967–68	83.17	5.67	−2.04	86.81	515.4	168.4
1968–69	82.26	3.82	−0.46	85.62	527.0	162.5
1969–70	87.06	3.55	−1.12	89.49	538.9	166.1
1970–71	94.87	2.01	−2.57	94.31	551.2	171.1
1971–72	92.02	−0.50	4.69	96.22	563.5	171.0
1972–73	84.90	3.59	0.31	88.79	575.9	154.2
1973–74	91.58	4.83	0.40	96.81	588.3	164.6
1974–75	87.35	7.38	−5.56	89.17	600.8	148.4
1975–76	105.91	6.44	−10.63	101.71	613.3	165.8
1976–77	97.62	0.39	1.47	99.49	625.8	159.0
1977–78	109.9	−1.00	−0.10	108.8	630.7	172.5

Source: Government of India, Ministry of Agriculture and Irrigation, Directorate of Economics and Statistics, *Bulletin on Food Statistics, 1978*, 28th issue (Delhi: Controller of Publications, 1979), table 11, pp. 124, 126. Data for production are for crop years; imports, stock movements, and population are for the following calendar years.
a. Gross production minus 12.5 percent for seed, feed, and waste.
b. Minus (−) denotes net exports.
c. Minus (−) denotes additions to stocks.

How Much Undernutrition?

Even in normal years, the diet of the average Indian barely meets the minimum requirement of about 2,100 calories per day estimated to be necessary for a population with the physical characteristics and age composition of India's.[2] The average per capita foodgrain consumption derived from the official Indian government food balance sheets accounts for about 1,500 calories per day.[3] Other foods supply an additional 550 calories (see table 1-1), for a total of 2,050 calories.

There is reason to believe that the official statistics understate actual foodgrain production, though this downward bias is partly offset by an inadequate allowance for postharvest losses.[4] On balance, net foodgrain availabilities derived from the official statistics probably still understate actual foodgrain consumption, perhaps by as much as 10 percent.[5] Even so, the daily food consumption of the average Indian would not exceed 2,250–2,300 calories.

NSS Estimates

Indications of the extent of undernutrition can be obtained from the National Sample Survey of household expenditures, which is taken an-

2. Minimum nutritional requirements vary a great deal depending on age, sex, stature, climate, and degree of physical activity. Estimates also depend on the standard applied. The average per capita level of 2,100 calories used here is intermediate between the minimum standard of 1,900 calories used by some nutritionists (1.5 times the basal metabolic rate [BMR]) and the 2,210 calorie requirement recommended for India in *The Fourth World Food Survey*, Food and Agriculture Organization of the United Nations (Rome: FAO, 1977), app. C, p. 78. The "critical limit" for India (1.2 times BMR) is stated by FAO to be 1,486 calories (app. M, p. 127).

3. The caloric conversion factor used in this chapter is that implicit in the FAO food balances: 1 kilogram of foodgrains = 3,285 calories.

4. The official food balances allow 3 percent for waste, but a survey by an expert committee appointed by the government of India in 1966 places losses in threshing, transit, and processing and postharvest losses to rodents and insects at 9.33 percent of gross production. See S. K. Ray, "Foodgrains Demand and Supply: Projection of Regional Imbalance," *Economic and Political Weekly*, Review of Agriculture, June 26, 1971, p. A-63.

5. This is a rough estimate, based on the widely held belief that actual consumption is somewhere within the range between average availabilities, as indicated by the official statistics based on food balance sheets, and those shown by consumer expenditure surveys conducted by the National Sample Survey Organization. The NSS data have run about 20 percent above the official data.

nually and covers all of India, and from nutritional surveys. The NSS data on foodgrain consumption in 1964–65, by expenditure groups, are shown in table 6-2.[6] These data indicate that about 15 percent of the total population, the same percentage of the rural population, and almost half of the urban population consume less than 160 kilograms of foodgrains per capita, which is generally considered a minimum level for adequate nutrition (160 kilograms of foodgrains supply about 1,440 calories per day). Urban foodgrain consumption is lower than rural consumption in all expenditure classes.

The table also suggests implausibly high consumption levels in the upper brackets, particularly in the rural areas.[7] The NSS data clearly overstate actual consumption in these brackets, probably because they include food given to servants and laborers who are not counted as members of the household. It is likely, in turn, that consumption in the lower brackets is understated to the extent that it does not include food received from employers. This flaw impairs the usefulness of the NSS in assessing the extent of undernutrition.[8]

In 1964–65, the average per capita foodgrain consumption derived from the NSS (205.5 kilograms) was 17 percent higher than the average foodgrain consumption derived from the official food balances (175.3 kilograms).[9]

Quantities of other foods by income groups are not shown in the NSS, but it is possible to arrive at a rough approximation of the calories contributed by these foods.

Authors' Estimates

The following procedure has been used here: first, expenditures on foods other than foodgrains were totaled separately for foods of vegetable origin (roots, vegetables, fruits, nuts, sugar, and edible oil) and foods of animal origin (dairy products, meat, eggs, and fish) (see appendix tables A-4 and A-5). Then, the pattern by expenditure groups

6. The year 1964–65 was chosen because it was a year in which food supplies were relatively ample and because foodgrain consumption for that year is shown in terms of quantities as well as rupee expenditures.

7. In the top rural bracket 417 kilograms of foodgrain per day would be equivalent to about 3,800 calories per day. To this must be added about 2,000 calories from other foods (see table 6-4), for a total of 5,800 calories per day.

8. It also impairs somewhat its usefulness as a basis for projecting per capita demand. See chapter 7.

9. See table 6-1. Similar or even greater differences can be found for other years.

Table 6-2. *Annual Per Capita Consumption of Foodgrains, by Expenditure Class, India, 1964–65*

Expenditure class (rupees per year)	Total population		Rural population		Urban population	
	Percent in class	Foodgrain consumption (kilograms per year)	Percent in class	Foodgrain consumption (kilograms per year)	Percent in class	Foodgrain consumption (kilograms per year)
0–96	1.3	80.3	1.5	81.8	0.5	63.1
96–132	4.6	116.3	5.1	118.7	2.3	93.4
132–156	5.2	139.9	5.8	143.2	3.0	113.5
156–180	6.8	153.3	7.3	158.4	4.9	120.9
180–216	11.6	174.0	12.1	180.8	9.4	137.2
216–252	12.3	188.8	12.8	196.9	10.0	145.0
252–288	11.2	211.7	11.6	222.8	9.7	155.4
288–336	11.8	217.7	11.8	230.8	11.5	160.8
336–408	12.7	233.8	12.5	250.5	13.6	168.4
408–516	10.0	248.0	9.6	269.1	11.4	172.0
516–660	6.0	265.3	5.2	303.2	9.3	174.2
660–900	3.7	264.1	2.8	322.1	7.6	172.6
900 and above	2.8	302.1	1.9	417.1	6.9	170.4
All classes	100.0	205.5	100.0	217.2	100.0	156.1
Average total consumer expenditure (rupees per year)		344		322		438[a]

Source: Government of India, Cabinet Secretariat, *The National Sample Survey, Tables with Notes on Consumer Expenditure*, 19th Round: July 1964–June 1965, no. 192 (Delhi: Manager of Publications, 1972), table 1.3.0, pp. 18–20; table 1.5.0, p. 29; table 1.6.0, pp. 30–31; table 2.3.0, pp. 60–62; table 2.5.0, p. 70; table 2.6.0, pp. 71–72. Total population figures based on weighted urban and rural data.

a. The higher average expenditure in urban areas does not necessarily imply higher real income. Food prices, in particular, tend to be higher in the cities.

Table 6-3. *Calories Derived from Foodgrains, Other Foods of Vegetable Origin, and Foods of Animal Origin, by Expenditure Class, Total Population, India, 1975*
Calories per capita per day

Expenditure class (rupees per year)ᵃ	Percent of sample	Foodgrainsᵇ	Other vegetable foodsᶜ	Animal foodsᵈ	Total calories
0–96	1.3	589	94	7	690
96–132	4.6	853	152	13	1,018
132–156	5.2	1,026	173	19	1,218
156–180	6.8	1,125	213	27	1,365
180–216	11.6	1,277	254	34	1,565
216–252	12.3	1,385	302	51	1,738
252–288	11.2	1,553	369	71	1,993
288–336	11.8	1,597	418	87	2,102
336–408	12.7	1,716	500	119	2,335
408–516	10.0	1,819	611	162	2,592
516–660	6.0	1,946	768	227	2,941
660–900	3.7	1,937	997	315	3,249
900 and above	2.8	2,216	1,738	465	4,419
All classesᵈ	100.0	1,507	436	102	2,045

Source: *National Sample Survey*, 19th Round; converted to caloric consumption for 1975 on the basis of United Nations Food and Agriculture Organization caloric consumption data (see table 1-1). Total population figures based on weighted urban and rural data (see the appendix for per capita expenditure on foods other than foodgrains, 1964–65).

a. Rupees of 1964–65 purchasing power.

b. Calories derived from foodgrains in each class based on ratio to average of all classes in table 6-2.

c. Assumes calories derived from these foods are the same percentage of average for all classes as expenditures on these foods.

d. From table 1-1. Average expenditure is 344 rupees per year.

was applied to the 1975 national average number of calories derived from vegetable foods other than foodgrains and from foods of animal origin (see table 1-1).[10] For foodgrains, the distribution of quantities consumed in 1964–65 (table 6-2) was adjusted to the national average calories derived from foodgrains for 1975 (table 1-1). The results are shown in tables 6-3 to 6-5.

One conclusion emerging from the tables is that the average urban consumer eats 452 calories less in the form of foodgrains than his rural counterpart but makes up for it to a large extent by consuming 243 more calories in the form of other vegetable foods and 73 more calories in foods

10. The implicit assumption here is that calories derived from "other foods" in the rural and urban population and in each expenditure class bear the same relation to the national average of calories derived from these foods as expenditure on these foods to national average expenditures.

Table 6-4. *Calories Derived from Foodgrains, Other Foods of Vegetable Origin, and Foods of Animal Origin, by Expenditure Class, Rural Population, India, 1975*
Calories per capita per day

Expenditure class (rupees per year)[a]	Percent of sample	Foodgrains[b]	Other vegetable foods[c]	Animal foods[c]	Total calories
0–96	1.5	598	90	7	695
96–132	5.1	869	145	13	1,027
132–156	4.8	1,048	164	17	1,229
156–180	7.3	1,159	201	26	1,386
180–216	12.1	1,324	239	32	1,595
216–252	12.8	1,440	282	49	1,771
252–288	11.6	1,631	350	67	2,048
288–336	11.8	1,689	390	84	2,163
336–408	12.5	1,833	461	115	2,409
408–516	9.6	1,970	566	155	2,691
516–660	5.2	2,220	700	217	3,137
660–900	2.8	2,357	924	305	3,586
900 and above	1.9	3,053	1,479	404	4,936
All classes[d]	100.0	1,593	388	88	2,069

Source: Same as table 6-3.
a. Rupees of 1964–65 purchasing power.
b. Calories derived from foodgrains in each class based on ratio to average of all classes in table 6-2.
c. Assumes calories derived from these foods are the same percentage of average for all classes as expenditures on these foods.
d. Average expenditure is 322 rupees per year.

of animal origin. His total intake of 1,933 calories per day is, however, 136 calories less than the rural average. This result is probably reliable.[11]

Table 6-3 also suggests that over half the population falls short of the minimum requirement of 2,100 calories. This result, however, must be interpreted with caution. There are several reasons for believing that actual calorie consumption by the lower income groups is greater than would appear from the data.

First, as pointed out earlier, there is reason to believe that the national average food consumption derived from the official production statistics, to which these calculations are keyed, probably understates actual food supplies, perhaps by as much as 10 percent. If total calorie consumption

11. It is possible, however, that our procedure overstates the calories derived from "other foods" by the urban population in comparison with the rural population, to the extent that the prices of these foods are higher in the cities.

Table 6-5. *Calories Derived from Foodgrains, Other Foods of Vegetable Origin, and Foods of Animal Origin, by Expenditure Class, Urban Population, India, 1975*
Calories per capita per day

Expenditure class (rupees per year)[a]	Percent of sample	Foodgrains[b]	Other vegetable foods[c]	Animal foods[c]	Total calories
0–96	0.5	461	123	6	590
96–132	2.3	684	184	18	886
132–156	3.0	830	221	31	1,082
156–180	4.9	884	271	34	1,189
180–216	9.4	1,003	309	46	1,358
216–252	10.0	1,060	377	67	1,504
252–288	9.7	1,137	437	88	1,662
288–336	11.5	1,176	508	106	1,790
336–408	13.6	1,231	615	137	1,983
408–516	11.4	1,258	727	188	2,173
516–660	9.3	1,274	897	254	2,425
660–900	7.6	1,262	1,081	334	2,677
900 and above	6.9	1,246	1,580	539	3,365
All classes[d]	100.0	1,141	631	161	1,933

Source: Same as table 6-3.
a. Rupees of 1964–65 purchasing power.
b. Calories derived from foodgrains in each class based on ratio to average of all classes in table 6-2.
c. Assumes calories derived from these foods are the same percentage of average for all classes as expenditures on these foods.
d. Average expenditure is 438 rupees per year.

in each class is raised by 10 percent, about 12 to 15 percent of the population would shift above the 2,100 calorie dividing line.

Second, food expenditures for the three upper income classes, particularly in the rural sector, overstate per capita consumption because, as already noted, they include food given to employees, who are not counted as members of the household. Actual calorie consumption per capita in the affluent classes probably does not exceed 3,000 calories. Distribution of the "excess" calories over the lower half of the population would add about 100 calories per capita to average consumption in these classes.

Third, the procedure used here to translate expenditures on foods other than foodgrains into calories undoubtedly leads to an underestimate of the calories that poor people derive from such foods: low-income consumers will tend to purchase cheap foods with high energy content.

All these considerations lead to the conclusion that between one-third and two-fifths of the population—rather than one-half—fall short of the 2,100 calorie minimum in a normal year.[12] This proportion may, however, rise to over 40 percent in years of severe crop shortfalls. Similar adjustments for the rural and urban populations suggest that the percentage of the urban population consuming less than 2,100 calories is somewhat higher (45 percent) than for the rural population (35 percent).

It is interesting to compare these results with those of three nutritional surveys.

Three Nutritional Surveys

Table 6-6 is based on a study of food consumption in Calcutta in 1969–70.[13] This nutritional survey suggests an even lower average calorie intake than that we derived from the NSS data (adjusted to the national average based on the official production statistics) for the urban population (table 6-5), although the calories derived from foodgrains are higher. Calories derived from foods other than foodgrains average only 400, as compared with about 800 in our estimate. Eighty-seven percent of the persons included in the Calcutta sample show an average caloric intake of less than 2,100 calories.

A diet survey carried out by the National Nutrition Monitoring Bureau covering nine states provides information on average caloric intake per consumption unit (male adult equivalent) for three broad income groups.[14] Table 6-7 shows this information for rural households,[15] as well as the same data adjusted to an average per capita basis. Like the Calcutta sample, the NNMB sample shows a lower average calorie intake and a much higher percentage of the sample (over 97 percent in this case) falling below the 2,100 calorie minimum than the data derived from the adjusted NSS rural data (table 6-4).

In 1971–72, the National Sample Survey Organization collected detailed information on food consumption from nationwide rural and urban samples at the request of the Food and Agriculture Organization of the

12. This conclusion is based on an upward adjustment of 10 percent, plus 100 calories for the classes below 2,100 calories.

13. Hindustan Thompson Associates Ltd., for U.S. Agency for International Development, *A Study of Food Habits in Calcutta* (Calcutta: Hindustan Thompson for USAID, 1972).

14. National Nutrition Monitoring Bureau, *Report for the Period Ending 31st August 1974* (Hyderabad, India: National Institute of Nutrition and the Indian Council of Medical Research, 1975). The survey was carried out in 1973–74.

15. Results for urban households were not available.

Table 6-6. *Average Daily Per Capita Intake of Calories, by Expenditure Class, Calcutta, 1969–70*

Expenditure class (rupees per year)	Percent of sample	Total calories	Source of calories	
			Foodgrains	Other foods
Less than 180	4.6	1,162	1,148[a]	88[a]
180–240	5.7	1,296		
240–360	12.6	1,345	1,288[b]	158[b]
360–480	15.6	1,528		
480–720	21.3	1,677	1,372	305
720–960	12.0	1,864	1,393[c]	497[c]
960–1,200	10.9	1,918		
1,200–1,500	4.7	2,045	1,372[d]	868[d]
1,500–1,800	4.2	2,122		
1,800–2,100	1.9	2,145		
2,100–2,400	2.6	2,261		
2,400–3,000	1.4	2,320		
3,000–3,600	1.0	2,696		
3,600–4,800	0.8	2,952		
Over 4,800	0.7	2,658		
All classes	100.0	1,724	1,330	394

Source: Hindustan Thompson Associates Ltd. for U.S. Agency for International Development, *A Study of Food Habits in Calcutta* (Calcutta: Hindustan Thompson for USAID, 1972), p. 20, and tables A-60, p. 76; A-65, p. 81; and A-69, p. 85. Data include meals taken outside the home by regular members of the household. Household employees are excluded.
a. Expenditure of less than 240 rupees per year.
b. Expenditure of 240–480 rupees per year.
c. Expenditure of 720–1,200 rupees per year.
d. Expenditure of over 1,200 rupees per year.

Table 6-7. *Average Daily Calorie Intake of the Rural Population of Nine States,[a] by Income, India, 1970s*

Income per capita (rupees per year)	Percent of households in sample	Calorie intake per consumption unit[b]	Calorie intake per capita[c]
Under 365	61.5	2,046	1,637
365–730	24.9	2,306	1,845
730–1,825	11.1	2,455	1,964
0–1,825[d]	97.5	2,159	1,727

Source: National Nutrition Monitoring Bureau, *Report for the Period Ending 31st August 1974* (Hyderabad, India: National Institute of Nutrition and the Indian Council of Medical Research, 1975), tables 2, 4.
a. Kerala, Tamil Nadu, Karnataka, Andhra Pradesh, Maharashtra, Gujarat, Madhya Pradesh, West Bengal, Uttar Pradesh.
b. The NNMB *Report*, table 4, state averages weighted on the basis of share of rural population of each state in total for nine states.
c. Ratio of average per capita calorie intake to average adult male intake (0.8). Based on Government of India, Ministry of Planning, Department of Statistics, National Sample Survey Organization, *The National Sample Survey*, 26th Round: July 1971–June 1972, *Calorie and Protein Content of Food Items Consumed per Diem per Consumer Unit, All-India, Rural*, no. 258/10 (NSSO, 1976).
d. Those with incomes over 1,825 rupees per year were not included in the results.

United Nations.[16] The published data show calories derived from five major food groups,[17] as well as total calorie and protein consumption, by expenditure groups. Consumption is shown per consumer unit, but it is possible to convert this into average per capita consumption, since the survey shows the number of persons as well as the number of consumer units per household.[18]

The results of the survey, summarized in tables 6-8 and 6-9, are similar to those derived by us in tables 6-4 and 6-5. Average calorie consumption levels are about 100 calories lower for the urban population (2,049) than for the rural population (2,168); both are close to the minimum nutritional standard of 2,100 calories. Calories derived from the principal staples (mainly foodgrains) make up the bulk of the diet; foods of animal origin account for only 7.4 percent of the total caloric intake in the cities and less than 5 percent in the countryside. The distribution by expenditure groups is also similar, but here again, the calorie levels shown in the survey are implausibly low in the lowest expenditure brackets and implausibly high in the highest brackets, particularly in the rural areas. From the survey it would appear that about 35 percent of the rural population and about half of the urban population consume less than the 2,100 calorie minimum.

How Reliable Are the Surveys?

The reliability of the surveys depends on the accuracy and completeness of the individual returns and on how representative the samples are. As already indicated, the NSS data seem to be flawed by the inclusion of food given to employees of affluent households who are not counted as members of the household. But the NSS sample (a large, two-stage random sample) may be expected to be more representative of the population as a whole than the Calcutta and NNMB samples.

16. Government of India, Ministry of Planning, Department of Statistics, National Sample Survey Organization, *The National Sample Survey*, 26th Round: July 1971–June 1972, *Calorie and Protein Content of Food Items Consumed per Diem per Consumer Unit, All-India, Rural*, no. 258/10 (NSSO, 1976); and *All-India, Urban*, no. 258/11 (NSSO, 1976).

17. For the food groups, see table 6-8, note a. This breakdown makes it difficult to compare the results with production data on foodgrains, which include pulses but not potatoes or sugar.

18. Consumer units are male adult equivalents. The relation between consumer units per household and persons per household varies according to the age-sex composition of the household members, which, in turn, varies with income; but the averages in each income group cluster rather closely around a general average of 0.8 for both rural and urban populations.

Table 6-8. *Average Daily Consumption of Calories per Capita, by Expenditure Class, Rural Population, India, 1971–72*

| Expenditure class (rupees per year) | Composition of class | | | Calories consumed | | | | | | |
| | Number of persons | Number of consumer units | Percent of sample, persons | Per consumer unit | Per capita | Per capita, by food group[a] | | | | |
						I	II	III	IV	V
Less than 180	2,811	2,216	4.6	1,493	1,176	1,051	61	14	23	27
180–252	7,206	5,721	11.9	1,957	1,436	1,266	74	24	35	36
252–288	4,902	3,886	8.1	2,287	1,814	1,588	99	35	48	43
288–336	6,692	5,295	11.0	2,431	1,923	1,646	117	53	54	52
336–408	9,736	7,761	16.1	2,734	2,179	1,848	138	69	68	56
408–516	10,667	8,518	17.6	3,127	2,495	2,060	165	106	86	77
516–660	8,441	6,752	13.9	3,513	2,810	2,256	219	151	101	82
660–900	6,015	4,880	9.9	4,016	3,257	2,488	301	219	128	122
900–1200	2,434	1,979	4.0	4,574	3,719	2,744	361	312	160	142
Over 1200	1,697	1,369	2.8	6,181	4,988	3,294	496	565	257	376
All classes	60,601	49,198	100.0	2,724	2,168	1,787	159	99	75	48

Source: Government of India, Ministry of Planning, Department of Statistics, National Sample Survey Organization, *The National Sample Survey*, 26th Round: July 1971–June 1972, *Calorie and Protein Content of Food Items Consumed per Diem per Consumer Unit, All-India, Rural*, no. 258/10 (NSSO, 1976). Figures are rounded.

a. Food groups: I: cereals, potatoes, sugar, jaggery, and cereal substitutes; II: pulses, nuts, and seeds; III: milk and milk products, meat, eggs, and fish; IV: edible oils; V: fruits, vegetables, spices, and prepared food.

Table 6-9. Average Daily Consumption of Calories per Capita, by Expenditure Class, Urban Population, India, 1971–72

Expenditure class (rupees per year)	Composition of class			Calories consumed						
	Number of persons	Number of consumer units	Percent of sample, persons	Per consumer unit	Per capita	Per capita, by food group[a]				
						I	II	III	IV	V
Less than 180	1,104	872	1.2	1,228	970	845	33	20	32	41
180–252	4,784	3,763	5.2	1,582	1,245	1,064	52	32	46	52
252–288	4,397	3,495	4.8	1,821	1,448	1,219	70	42	62	56
288–336	7,135	5,680	7.8	1,970	1,568	1,296	77	52	74	70
336–408	11,852	9,482	13.0	2,130	1,704	1,366	95	73	88	81
408–516	16,060	12,900	17.6	2,343	1,874	1,456	114	103	94	108
516–660	15,125	12,210	16.6	2,622	2,124	1,564	145	142	145	129
660–900	14,045	11,408	15.4	2,872	2,332	1,593	163	209	184	183
900–1,200	7,842	6,516	8.5	3,190	2,648	1,632	183	260	229	344
Over 1,200	9,092	7,636	9.9	3,750	3,150	1,614	225	412	315	584
All classes	91,436	74,139	100.0	2,539	2,049	1,456	131	152	134	176

Source: Same as table 6-8, *All-India, Urban*, no. 258/11 (1976). Figures are rounded.
a. Food groups are as defined in table 6-8.

To get a rough idea of differences in the composition of the various samples by income groups, we compared the Calcutta sample for 1969–70 with the NSS sample of Calcutta households for 1970–71.[19] We also compared the NNMB sample with the NSS sample of rural households. The comparisons show a much heavier representation of poor households in the Calcutta and NNMB surveys.[20] This helps to explain the lower average calorie intake and the higher percentage of undernourished people in these surveys. The Calcutta survey, and possibly the other surveys as well, is flawed also by (inadvertent) underreporting of nonstaple foods.

19. Government of India, Ministry of Planning, Department of Statistics, National Sample Survey Organization, *The National Sample Survey,* 25th Round: July 1970–June 1971, *Table with Notes on Consumer Expenditure,* no. 269 (NSSO, 1975).

20. The Calcutta nutritional sample shows 38.5 percent of households with incomes below 480 rupees per year, compared with about 15 percent in the 1970–71 NSS sample for Calcutta. The NNMB sample shows 61.5 percent of households below 365 rupees per year, compared with about 43 percent in the rural NSS sample for 1970–71 and 38 percent in 1971–72.

CHAPTER SEVEN

India's Food Demand at a Population of One Billion

DEMAND PROJECTIONS may be based either on nutritional requirements or on market demand. In the first case, the quantity of cereals,
pulses, and other food that would satisfy an individual's minimum need
for calories, proteins, and other nutrients is specified in advance and future requirements are estimated as a function of population growth alone.
The diet that would meet the nutritional needs may be determined in two
ways. It may be based on a minimum-cost balanced diet for everyone;
this would presuppose a revolutionary equalization of incomes or comprehensive food rationing or both. Alternatively, planners could ensure
that the minimum nutritional requirements of the poor were met by a
system of subsidized food distribution, while assuming that the more
affluent would cover—or supplement—their food needs in the free
market. Such exercises, however, are rather academic in that they postu-
late what ought to be rather than estimating what is likely to be the demand for food in the coming decades.

Factors Affecting Demand

In what follows it is assumed that the demand for food in India will
continue to be determined in a market which is essentially free, although
a small proportion of the total foodgrain supply—about 10 percent—
will be distributed through fair-price shops to enable the urban poor to
meet their most essential food needs at slightly lower prices, particularly
in years of foodgrain shortage (see chapter 4). In a free market, the
growth of demand for food is determined mainly by population growth,

the growth of per capita incomes, and the income elasticity of demand (which changes with the level of income). Additional factors that may affect the demand for food include the degree of urbanization, the distribution of income, and real prices of food.

The demand projections in this study focus on foodgrains, which are predominant in the Indian diet and may be expected to supply the bulk of the calories through the remainder of this century. However, separate projections are made for other foods whose relative importance may be expected to increase with rising incomes. An allowance is also made for seed and postharvest losses.

Population Growth

Most projections of foodgrain consumption consider only the growth of total population and of average incomes. This may be misleading in countries experiencing a rapid rate of urbanization. In India, the rapidly growing urban population shows distinctly lower levels of foodgrain consumption at comparable incomes (see table 6-2) as well as lower income elasticities. This is partly offset, however, by higher levels of demand for other foods (see tables 6-4 and 6-5). Consequently, a differential rate of growth of rural and urban populations will affect total demand.

Between 1951 and 1961 the annual compound rate of growth of India's population was 2.1 percent. During the 1960s it increased to 2.2 percent. There are indications, however, that population growth is slowing down. There are several reasons for this. First, with the rapid development of health services in India, the mortality rate will begin to level off. Second, fertility rates have been declining: between 1968 and 1975, the total fertility rate (children per 1,000 families) declined by 8 percent, from 5,671 to 5,241.[1] Third, fertility rates are substantially lower in urban areas than in rural areas, a fact that will reduce the birthrate as more people migrate to the cities (table 7-1). For the purposes of this projection, we have assumed that India's rate of population growth, which was running at 2.14 percent in 1971–76,[2] will decline from 2.1 percent in the 1970s to 2.0 percent in the 1980s and 1.9 percent in the 1990s.[3]

1. See Amy Ong Tsui and Donald J. Bogue, "Declining World Fertility: Trends, Causes, Implications," *Population Bulletin,* vol. 33 (October 1978), pp. 14, 47.
2. Government of India, Planning Commission, *Draft Five Year Plan, 1978–83* (Delhi: Controller of Publications, 1978), p. 49.
3. This may be compared with World Bank projections, under the low fertility assumption, of 2.0 percent for 1971–81, 1.8 percent for 1981–91, and 1.6 percent for 1991–2001. The Population Division of the UN Secretariat gives low variant popula-

Table 7-1. *Age-Specific Fertility Rates, India, 1964–65, 1969, and 1972*

Age group	1964–65		1969		1972	
	Rural	Urban	Rural	Urban	Rural	Urban
15–19	83.2	67.5	97.9	78.8	97.2	52.2
20–24	247.2	251.9	261.9	244.7	273.5	220.6
25–29	241.3	271.5	266.9	252.6	283.4	247.3
30–34	195.4	195.1	226.0	212.6	227.2	173.4
35–39	177.5	130.1	158.3	140.4	151.2	108.2
40–44	79.1	12.1	77.1	69.6	82.7	43.3
45–49	33.1	8.5	35.5	38.3	32.7	13.0

Sources: Government of India, Cabinet Secretariat, *National Sample Survey,* Tables with Notes on *Differential Fertility and Mortality Rates in Rural and Urban Areas of India,* 19th Round: July 1964– June 1965, no. 186 (New Delhi, n.d.); U.S. Census Bureau, unpublished data, based on Government of India, Office of the Registrar General, *Sample Registration System Analytical Series,* no. 2 (1972); India, Office of the Registrar General, Vital Statistics Division, *Fertility Differentials in India: Results of the Fertility Survey in a Sub-Sample of SRS (1972)* (New Delhi, 1976), table 4, p. 6.

The 1961 census shows India's urban population at 79 million, with a growth rate of 2.5 percent during the decade 1951–61, as compared with 2.1 percent for the total population. During 1961–70 the annual rate of growth of the urban population was 3.3 percent—rather slow, compared with most other third world countries[4]—while the rate of increase of the total population was only 2.2 percent. Since we believe that the trend toward industrialization and urbanization is likely to continue despite the increased emphasis on rural development in current government planning, we have assumed a slight acceleration of the annual rate of growth of the urban population, from an estimated 4 percent in the 1970s to 4.5 percent in the 1980s and 5 percent in the 1990s. It is likely, however, that much of this growth will be in smaller urban centers. The resulting population projections (table 7-2) show a 63 percent increase in total population, but a tripling of the urban population between 1975 and 2000, with the share of the urban population increasing from 22 percent to 41 percent.

tion projections that are similar to the World Bank projections, but their medium variant estimates are higher (2.4 percent and 1.9 percent). The most recent official Indian projections (*Draft Five Year Plan, 1978–83,* p. 49), on the other hand, are more optimistic than ours (1.97 percent for 1976–81, 1.79 percent for 1981–86, and 1.66 percent for 1986–91).

4. The average rate of urban population growth in developing countries was estimated as 4.1 percent for the period 1960–80, by the United Nations, Department of Economic and Social Affairs, in *Growth of the World's Urban and Rural Population, 1920–2000,* Population Studies no. 44, ST/SOA/Series A/44 (New York: UN, 1969), p. 64.

Table 7-2. *Population of India, 1960–70, and Projections for 1975–2000*
Millions

Year	Rural	Urban	Total	Urban as percent of total
1960	360	79	439	18
1970	439	109	548	20
1975	476	135	611	22
1980	514	161	675	24
1990	572	250	822	30
2000	586	407	993	41
Index of population (1975 = 100)				
1960	75.6	58.5	71.8	...
1970	92.2	80.7	89.7	...
1975	100.0	100.0	100.0	...
1980	108.0	119.3	110.5	...
1990	120.2	185.2	134.5	...
2000	123.1	301.5	162.5	...

Sources: 1960–70, Government of India, Office of the Registrar General, and World Bank; 1975–2000, authors' projections.

Income Growth

The national income of India grew by 4.1 percent annually (at constant prices) during the second plan period (1956–57 to 1960–61), 2.6 percent during the Third Plan period (1961–62 to 1965–66), 4.4 percent during the annual plans (1966–67 to 1968–69), and 3.0 percent during the Fourth Plan period (1969–70 to 1973–74). For the period 1960–74, the average was 3.5 percent.[5]

The target for the Fifth Plan, 1974–75 to 1978–79, was 5.5 percent a year, but actual performance fell short of the goal. In the first year of the plan, real national income grew by less than 1 percent, partly as a result of the poor harvest, a low rate of growth of savings and investment, and the oil crisis. By 1975–76, however, it appeared that the effects of the oil price increase had been largely absorbed. Inflation was being brought under control, foodgrain production reached an all-time high of 121 million tons, output of electricity, coal, and fertilizers resumed their upward trend, and real national income increased by 8.5 percent—the largest increase achieved in any single year. The rate of economic growth dropped back to 1.6 percent in 1976–77, but recovered to 5 percent in 1977–78, giving an average of 5 percent for those three years.

In our projections, we have assumed that real national income will have

5. World Bank figures.

increased by 4.7 percent annually in the second half of the 1970s, for an average growth of 3.3 percent for the decade. Total income growth is projected to accelerate to 5.2 percent in the 1980s and to 6.3 percent in the 1990s. Per capita income growth, which was virtually nil during the first half of the 1970s, will have recovered, to 2.7 percent, in the second half, and then will rise to 3.2 percent in the 1980s and to 4.4 percent in the 1990s (see table 7-3). Average per capita incomes for the base period were broken down into rural and urban averages on the basis of the ratio of rural to urban per capita expenditure obtained from the National Sample Survey, 19th Round, 1964–65. For subsequent years we have assumed that rural incomes—which are, on the average, 27 percent lower than urban incomes—will rise at the same rate as urban incomes.[6]

Table 7-3. *Per Capita Income, India, 1970 and 1975, and Projections for 1980–2000*
Amounts in 1972 rupees. Index: 1975 = 100

	Rural		Urban		Total population	
Year	Amount	Index	Amount	Index	Amount	Index
1970	712	101	974	101	767	101
1975	705	100	964	100	758[a]	100
1980	797	113	1,089	113	867	114
1990	1,064	151	1,456	151	1,182	156
2000	1,572	223	2,150	223	1,809	239

Sources: 1970 total (average of 1968–69 to 1970–71), Agency for International Development, Statistics and Reports Division, *Gross National Product, by Region and Country* (AID, 1974); dollars converted to rupees at 7.5 to 1. Total for 1975, estimated based on GNP increase reported for the Fourth Plan period, 1969–70 to 1973–74. Rural-urban breakdown based on relative per capita expenditure levels, in Government of India, Cabinet Secretariat, *The National Sample Survey, Tables with Notes on Consumer Expenditure,* 24th Round: July 1968–June 1969, and 26th Round: July 1971–June 1972.
a. The *World Bank Atlas, 1977,* puts India's per capita GNP for 1975 at $140, or $109 in 1972 prices. This is about 2 percent of the U.S. per capita income. If purchasing power parity rates are used instead of exchange rates, the average Indian per capita income is over three times as high (6.28 percent of U.S. per capita income). This would give an average income of about $365 in 1972 prices (see *World Bank Atlas, 1976,* p. 21).

Base-Period Consumption

As pointed out in chapter 6, there is reason to believe that the average national food consumption derived from official production figures understates actual consumption, while the average consumption derived from the annual National Sample Survey probably overstates it. The analyst is faced with the dilemma of using data he knows to be distorted or at-

6. In estimating the future demand for food, per capita expenditure rather than per capita income is used as the basis. The growth of per capita expenditure, in turn, is assumed to be proportional to that of per capita income.

tempting to correct the distortions on the basis of more or less arbitrary assumptions concerning the nature and extent of bias in the data.

We opted for a pragmatic solution based on the adjusted NSS data derived in chapter 6. For the rural population, we adopted a base-year consumption pattern corresponding to the 322-rupee average expenditure level. For the urban population, we adopted the consumption pattern corresponding to the 438-rupee average expenditure level. The caloric consumption levels are interpolations read from freehand consumption functions based on tables 6-4 and 6-5. The base-year data for the total population are weighted averages of those for the rural and urban populations. The calories derived from foodgrains are then converted to kilograms of grain on the basis of a "no waste" conversion factor (see table 7-4).[7]

Per Capita Demand as a Function of Income[8]

The data in tables 6-4 and 6-5 can serve as a basis for estimating the relation between food consumption and incomes and, hence, the future demand at the projected higher income levels. For example, if we project average per capita urban expenditures to rise 123 percent by the end of the century, to 976 rupees, we can estimate urban food consumption in that year on the basis of the current consumption pattern for urban consumers at the 976 rupee expenditure level (see table 7-4).

To better visualize the relation between food consumption and incomes, the data are shown graphically in figures 7-1 and 7-2. A striking feature is the leveling-off of foodgrain consumption as incomes rise from the present average. In the urban areas (figure 7-2) there is no increase at all. At the income levels projected for the end of the century the urban population derives more calories from other foods of vegetable origin than it does from foodgrains. Though calories derived from foods of animal origin rise even more sharply with rising income, they continue to

---

7. One kilogram = 3,550 calories. From U.S. Department of Agriculture, Bureau of Human Nutrition and Home Economics, *Tables of Food Composition in Terms of Eleven Nutrients,* prepared in cooperation with the National Research Council, USDA, Misc. Pub. 572 (U.S. Government Printing Office, 1945), table 1, p. 16. (The factor used by FAO works out to 3,285 calories.) This procedure has two practical advantages: it yields base-year average caloric levels which we believe to be more realistic than those derived from the official food balance statistics; yet the use of the higher calorie conversion factor restores continuity with the familiar foodgrain production and consumption data.

8. Represented by expenditure in the NSS.

Table 7-4. *Consumption of Foodgrains, Other Foods of Vegetable Origin, and Foods of Animal Origin, India, 1975, and Projections for 1990 and 2000*

Item	Rural 1975	Rural 1990	Rural 2000	Urban 1975	Urban 1990	Urban 2000	Total population[a] 1975	Total population[a] 1990	Total population[a] 2000
Average expenditure level (1964–65 rupees)	322	486	718	438	661	976	344	537	822
Calories per capita per day	2,235	2,830	3,440	2,130	2,510	3,120	2,212	2,733	3,403
Foodgrains	1,730	2,040	2,300	1,240	1,250	1,230	1,621	1,800	1,858
Other vegetable foods	420	620	870	720	970	1,430	487	726	1,197
Animal foods	85	170	270	170	290	460	104	207	348
Foodgrain consumption per capita (kilograms per year)	178	210	236	127	129	126	167	185	191

Sources: Expenditure levels, 1975, from table 6-2; 1990 and 2000, projected on basis of income projections in table 7-3. Calories interpolated from freehand consumption functions based on tables 6-4 and 6-5. Foodgrain consumption, converted on the basis of 1 kilogram foodgrains = 3,550 calories.

a. Weighted average of rural and urban.

Figure 7-1. *Rural Food Consumption and Income, India, 1975, and Projections for 1990 and 2000*

Food consumption (calories per capita per day)

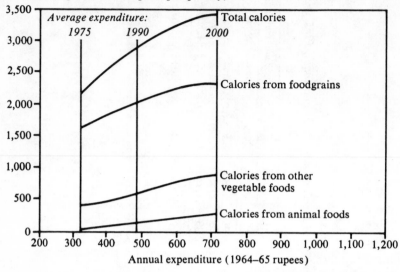

Source: Table 7-4.

Figure 7-2. *Urban Food Consumption and Income, India, 1975, and Projections for 1990 and 2000*

Food consumption (calories per capita per day)

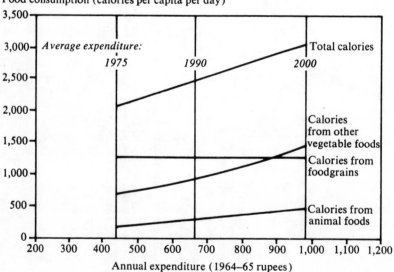

Source: Table 7-4.

represent only a small fraction of total consumption, particularly in the rural areas.[9]

Projected Demand for Foodgrains

We can now project the total demand for foodgrains for direct human consumption on the basis of population and income. As can be seen in table 7-5, direct human foodgrain consumption may be expected to rise

Table 7-5. *Demand for Foodgrains for Direct Human Consumption, India, 1975, and Projections for 1990 and 2000*

Year and item	Population		
	Rural	Urban	Total
1975			
Average per capita expenditure (1964–65 rupees per year)	322	438	344
Consumption per capita (calories per day)	1,730	1,240	1,621
Consumption per capita (kilograms per year)	178	127	167
Population (millions)	476	135	611
Total consumption (millions of metric tons per year)	84.7	17.1	101.8
1990			
Average per capita expenditure (1964–65 rupees per year)	486	661	537
Consumption per capita (calories per day)	2,040	1,250	1,800
Consumption per capita (kilograms per year)	210	129	185
Population (millions)	572	250	822
Total consumption (millions of metric tons per year)	120.1	32.2	152.3
2000			
Average per capita expenditure (1964–65 rupees per year)	718	976	822
Consumption per capita (calories per day)	2,300	1,230	1,858
Consumption per capita (kilograms per year)	236	126	191
Population (millions)	586	407	993
Total consumption (millions of metric tons per year)	138.3	51.3	189.6

Sources: Table 7-4; population from table 7-2.

9. The figures also illustrate the apparent upward bias of the data for the top income brackets, discussed earlier. Total calorie consumption would be expected to level off at about 3,000 calories (slightly more for the rural population, slightly less for the urban).

from 102 million tons in 1975 to 190 million tons by the end of the century. To this must be added requirements for seed, feed, and an allowance for losses in storage and processing, conventionally 12.5 percent of total production. While this may have been an adequate rule of thumb in the past, the proportion may be expected to change as a result of changes in the pattern of demand and production.

Seed and Feed Requirements

Seed requirements for foodgrains are shown in table 7-6 on the basis of projections of area under various crops and seeding rates per hectare. Seed requirements are expected to increase only slightly, from 6.4 million tons in 1975 to 7.0 million tons in 2000.

The demand for grains for animal feed will depend on the rate of increase in the consumption of dairy products and, to a minor extent, of meat. In 1975, dairy production accounted for almost all of the estimated 3 million tons of grain used for feed.[10] Future feed requirements are pro-

Table 7-6. *Seed Requirements for Foodgrains, India, 1975, and Projections for 1990 and 2000*

Crop	Seeding rates (kilograms of grain per hectare)	Sown area (millions of hectares)			Seed demand (millions of metric tons)		
		1975	1990	2000	1975	1990	2000
Rice	60	39.5	43.5	44.0	2.4	2.6	2.6
Wheat	110	20.4	24.7	25.0	2.2	2.7	2.7
Coarse grains	10	43.8	38.8	20.0	2.4	0.4	0.2
Pulses	55	24.5	26.0	27.7	1.4	1.4	1.5
All foodgrains	...	128.2	133.0	116.7	6.4	7.1	7.0

Sources: Seeding rates estimated from data in Government of India, Ministry of Agriculture and Irrigation, Directorate of Economics and Statistics, *Indian Agriculture in Brief*, 16th ed. (Delhi: Controller of Publications, 1978), table 3-2, p. 67; and Food and Agriculture Organization of the United Nations, *Indicative World Plan for Agricultural Development to 1975 and 1985*, Provisional Regional Study 4: *Asia and the Far East*, vol. 1 (Rome: FAO, 1968), pp. 243–52. Sown area from table 8-6.

10. Approximately 2.5 percent of total grain use; see Government of India, Ministry of Food and Agriculture, *Report of the Working Group for Formulation of Fourth Five-Year Plan Proposals on Demand Projections* (New Delhi, 1966), p. 6, cited in John R. Moore, Sardar S. Johl, and Ali M. Khusro, *Indian Foodgrain Marketing* (New Delhi: Prentice-Hall of India Private Ltd., 1973), p. 11.

jected on the basis of the anticipated demand for animal products, as follows: 1980, 4.0 million tons; 1990, 8.0 million tons; 2000, 16.3 million tons (see table 7-9).

On the other hand, we have ignored the demand for grain for meat production, on the following grounds. At present, the consumption of meat in India is very low (probably about 1.5 kilograms per capita per year)[11] and largely confined to goat and mutton, which consume no feed-grain. While per capita meat consumption may be expected to increase severalfold by the end of the century, it will still be very low and will undoubtedly continue to be based mainly on forage and waste products.

Postharvest Losses

In the absence of reliable data, we have derived postharvest losses for the base period as the residual between estimated disappearance in 1975–76 (trend value) and estimated consumption for food, seed, and feed. The residual amounts to 3.9 million tons, or 3.4 percent of food-grain production. For the sake of comparability, we have used the same percentage for future years, although it appears too low in the light of the 1966 findings of an Indian government expert committee.[12] A summary of the grain demand for seed and feed and estimated postharvest losses and the estimated total demand for all uses is presented in table 7-7.

Table 7-7. *Total Demand for Foodgrains, India, 1975, and Projections for 1990 and 2000*
Millions of metric tons

Use	1975	1990	2000
Direct human consumption	101.8	152.3	189.6
Seed	6.4	7.1	7.0
Feed	3.0	8.0	16.3
Waste	3.9[a]	5.9[b]	7.6[b]
Total	115.1[c]	173.3	220.5

Sources: Tables 7-5 and 7-6, and text, this chapter.
a. Residual.
b. Same percentage of total use as in 1975 (3.4 percent).
c. Trend value.

11. Based on Food and Agricultural Organization of the United Nations, unpublished data, for 1975 consumption.

12. See chapter 6, footnote 4.

NUU

Projected Demand for Other Foods

The demand for foods other than foodgrains is projected in tables 7-8 and 7-9. Total consumption of vegetable foods other than foodgrains may be expected to more than triple by the end of the century, from 31 million tons (grain equivalent) in 1975 to 112 million tons in 2000. This may be compared with the 86 percent rise in direct foodgrain consumption, from 102 million tons in 1975 to 190 million tons in 2000, projected in table 7-5. Total demand for foods of animal origin may be expected to rise even more sharply, to over five times the present (extremely low) level.

Table 7-8. *Demand for Vegetable Foods Other than Foodgrains, India, 1975, and Projections for 1990 and 2000*

	Population		
Year and item	Rural	Urban	Total
1975			
Average per capita expenditure (1964–65 rupees per year)	322	438	344
Consumption per capita (calories per day)	420	720	487
Consumption per capita (kilograms per year, grain equivalent)	43	74	50
Population (millions)	476	135	611
Total consumption (millions of metric tons per year, grain equivalent)	20.6	10.0	30.6
1990			
Average per capita expenditure (1964–65 rupees per year)	486	661	537
Consumption per capita (calories per day)	620	970	726
Consumption per capita (kilograms per year, grain equivalent)	64	100	75
Population (millions)	572	250	822
Total consumption (millions of metric tons per year, grain equivalent)	36.4	24.9	61.3
2000			
Average per capita expenditure (1964–65 rupees per year)	718	976	822
Consumption per capita (calories per day)	870	1,430	1,197
Consumption per capita (kilograms per year, grain equivalent)	89	147	123
Population (millions)	586	407	993
Total consumption (millions of metric tons per year, grain equivalent)	52.4	59.8	112.2

Sources: Table 7-4; population from table 7-2.

Table 7-9. *Demand for Foods of Animal Origin, India, 1975, and Projections for 1990 and 2000*

| Year and item | Population | | |
	Rural	Urban	Total
1975			
Average per capita expenditure (1964–65 rupees per year)	322	438	344
Consumption per capita (calories per day)	85	170	104
Population (millions)	476	135	611
Total consumption (trillions of calories)	14.8	8.4	23.2
Index of total consumption (1975 = 100)	100	100	100
1990			
Average per capita expenditure (1964–65 rupees per year)	486	661	537
Consumption per capita (calories per day)	170	290	207
Population (millions)	572	250	822
Total consumption (trillions of calories)	35.5	26.5	62.0
Index of total consumption (1975 = 100)	240	315	267
2000			
Average per capita expenditure (1964–65 rupees per year)	718	976	822
Consumption per capita (calories per day)	270	460	348
Population (millions)	586	407	993
Total consumption (trillions of calories)	57.8	68.3	126.1
Index of total consumption (1975 = 100)	390	813	544

Sources: Table 7-4; population from table 7-2.

Intercountry Comparison

To test the projections for plausibility, we have compared the food consumption levels projected for India for the years 1990 and 2000 with those prevailing in other Asian countries that have already reached income levels equal to or exceeding those projected for India for those years.[13] As can be seen from table 7-10, the projections for India seem rather high, particularly for the year 2000.[14] We have nevertheless accepted these estimates as a first approximation to a high estimate of future demand for food in India.

13. This comparison neglects differences in climate, physical characteristics, and age structure that affect calorie requirements.
14. This reflects the upward bias of the consumption estimates for the upper income classes, mentioned earlier.

Table 7-10. *Food Consumption in India Compared with That in Other Countries, 1975, and Projections for India, 1990 and 2000*

	Per capita income (U.S. dollars)	Calories per capita per day			
Country and year		Foodgrains	Other vege- table foods	Animal foods	Total
India					
1975	140	1,621	487	104	2,212
1990	234ª	1,800	726	207	2,733
2000	358ª	1,858	1,197	348	3,403
Thailand, 1975	350	1,709	500	173	2,382
Philippines, 1975	380	1,289	418	210	1,971
Republic of Korea, 1975	560	1,925	538	167	2,630
Malaysia, 1975	760	1,482	453	290	2,225
Egypt, 1975	260	1,875	608	154	2,637

Sources: Per capita income, *World Bank Atlas: Population, Per Capita Product, and Growth Rates, 1977* (World Bank, 1977), annex, pp. 27–28. Calories for India, tables 7-5, 7-8, and 7-9. Calories for other countries are for 1974, *Monthly Bulletin of Agricultural Economics and Statistics*, vol. 25 (April 1976).
a. In 1975 dollars. Based on table 7-3.

Projected Food Consumption under Alternative Assumptions

Table 7-11 illustrates the effect on the demand for food of alternative assumptions concerning population growth, income growth, and the degree of urbanization. Alternative A represents the food demand derived on the preceding pages. Alternative B assumes a lower population growth rate for the period 1990–2000 (1.5 percent instead of 2.0 percent). Alternative C assumes per capita income growth at half the rates assumed earlier. Alternative D assumes a constant proportion of urban residents (at 22 percent of total population) rather than a rising proportion (increasing to 41 percent in 2000). Alternative E shows what the hypothetical effect of a radical redistribution of incomes would have been on total food requirements in 1975.

Not surprisingly, a lower rate of population growth beginning in 1990 (alternative B) has only a marginal effect (4 percent) on the total population and, therefore, on total food requirements in the year 2000. Lower population growth rates would, however, have increasingly significant effects in the twenty-first century.

A lower rate of income growth (alternative C) would have substantial effects on the demand for food. The per capita demand for foodgrains in 2000 would be 13 percent less than under alternative A; the per capita

Table 7-11. *Effects of Alternative Assumptions on Projected Food Consumption, India, 1990 and 2000*

Alternative[a] and year	Per capita consumption				Total projected requirements			
	Foodgrains (kilograms per year)	Other vegetable foods per year, grain equivalent (kilograms)	Animal foods (calories per day)	Total (calories per day)	Foodgrains for human consumption (millions of metric tons)	Grain for feed, seed, and waste (millions of metric tons)	Other vegetable foods (millions of metric tons, grain equivalent)	Total[b] (millions of metric tons, grain equivalent)
Actual, 1975	167	50	104	2,212	101.8	13.3	30.6	145.7
Alternative A								
1990	185	75	207	2,733	152.3	21.0	61.3	234.6
2000	191	123	348	3,403	189.6	30.9	112.2	332.7
Alternative B								
1990	185	75	207	2,733	152.3	21.0	61.3	234.6
2000	191	123	348	3,403	182.2	29.6	107.7	319.5
Alternative C								
1990	165	60	176	2,495	135.6	18.3	49.3	203.2
2000	167	74	213	2,697	165.8	22.3	73.5	261.6
Alternative D								
1990	192	72	197	2,731	157.8	20.7	59.2	237.7
2000	212	102	312	3,326	210.5	29.8	101.3	341.6
Alternative C+D								
1990	171	57	166	2,507	140.6	18.4	46.9	205.9
2000	181	67	189	2,754	179.7	22.5	66.5	268.7
Alternative E								
1975	181	51	104	2,364	108.8	13.4	32.4	154.6

a. Alternatives: A: Authors' projections, tables 7-7 through 7-9. B: Lower population growth (1.5 percent instead of 2.0 percent) in 1990–2000. C: Lower per capita income growth (1.2 percent instead of 2.4 percent) for both rural and urban population in 1975–80; 1.5 percent instead of 3.0 percent in 1980–90; 2.0 percent instead of 4.0 percent in 1990–2000. D: Urban population constant at 22 percent instead of rising to 41 percent by 2000. E: With equalization of incomes. Based on table 6-3.
b. Includes animal products only in terms of the grain required for livestock feeding.

demand for other vegetable foods, 40 percent less; and the demand for calories from foods of animal origin, 39 percent less. Average calorie consumption would be 21 percent lower.[15] But even under this assumption, average food consumption would reach 2,500 calories in 1990 and 2,700 calories in the year 2000. Total foodgrain requirements would rise from 115 million tons in 1975 to 154 million tons in 1990 and 188 million tons in 2000 (as compared with 173 million tons and 220 million tons, respectively, under alternative A).

Alternative D, which assumes a stable rather than a rising proportion of urban dwellers, has only a slight effect on total food consumption but a marked effect on the composition of the diet. In 1990, foodgrain consumption per capita would be 4 percent higher than under alternative A, and 11 percent higher in 2000. Consumption of other vegetable foods would be 4 percent lower in 1990 and 17 percent lower in 2000. Consumption of foods of animal origin would be 5 percent lower in 1990 and 10 percent lower in 2000. Total foodgrain requirements would be 3 percent higher in 1990 and 9 percent higher in the year 2000.

Since a lower rate of urbanization is likely to be associated with lower average incomes, we have combined alternatives C and D to show their joint effects. This low-income scenario is treated below as the major alternative to the high-income alternative A.

Can Hunger Be Eliminated?

What are the implications of these projections for low-income groups? Can we expect hunger to be eliminated by the end of the century? The answer will depend on our assumptions about changes in the distribution of incomes. Hunger could be eliminated now if incomes were equalized. It is interesting to note that even such a radical redistribution would raise total food requirements by only 6 percent (alternative E); virtually the entire additional demand would be for foodgrains.

In most developing as well as developed countries, however, the distribution of incomes has proved to be remarkably resistant to change. In fact, the early stages of economic development frequently generate increased inequalities. In India, the available evidence suggests that there

15. This decline, however, is partly due to the fact that the data are less affected by upward statistical bias at the lower income levels assumed in alternative C than at the higher income levels in alternative A.

has been little change in the distribution of incomes in the past twenty years.[16] It seems realistic, therefore, to assume no significant change in the next twenty-five years. On this assumption, the incomes of low-income people would rise by the same percentage as the national average income.

We have estimated that, at present, between one-third and two-fifths of the population fall short of the 2,100 caloric minimum (see chapter 6). The spendable income necessary to ensure that minimum level of food consumption seems to be in the neighborhood of 250 rupees of 1964–65 purchasing power. If we accept the NSS data, about 40 percent of the population currently falls below that absolute poverty level of annual expenditures (table 6-3).

We have projected the average per capita income to rise 56 percent by 1990 and 139 percent by the end of the century from the 1975 base (table 7-3). If these increases apply equally to all expenditure classes, all but 11 percent of the population (those now in the three lowest expenditure groups) will have risen above the absolute poverty level by 1990, and all but about 5 percent (the lowest and most of the second-lowest group) will have crossed the poverty line by the year 2000.

If the rate of income growth turns out to be only half that projected here, about 20 percent of the population will still live in absolute poverty in 1990 and about 10 percent in the year 2000. In other words, the dimensions of the hunger problem may be expected to be substantially reduced in the normal course of economic development in the next twenty-five years, but it will not be completely eliminated without redistributive measures (such as food subsidies or income supplements) at the lower end of the income range.

These conclusions are subject to two qualifications. On one hand, it should be kept in mind that the projections may overstate both the number of undernourished people and the size of the per capita food deficit because of the apparent downward bias in the base-year data. On the other hand, it is possible that the favorable effects of income growth on food consumption by low-income groups could be nullified if real food

16. See Montek S. Ahluwalia, "Rural Poverty in India: 1956–57 to 1973–74," in *India: Occasional Papers,* World Bank Staff Working Paper 279 (World Bank, 1978), pp. 1–42; J. S. Sarma and Shyamal Roy, "Behavior of Foodgrains Production and Consumption in India, 1960–1977," draft discussion paper (International Food Policy Research Institute, 1978); P. K. Bardhan and T. N. Srinivasan, eds., *Poverty and Income Distribution in India* (Calcutta: Statistical Publishing Society, 1974); and V. M. Dandekar and Nilakantha Rath, "Poverty in India—I: Dimensions and Trends," *Economic and Political Weekly,* January 2, 1971, pp. 25–48.

prices should rise (as they did in the 1960s),[17] unless the price rise is offset by food subsidies.[18]

Interpretation of the Results

In interpreting these findings, the reader should bear in mind the limitations of the data and of the analytical method employed. The most important flaw in the data provided by the household expenditure surveys is the apparent statistical bias, which overstates food consumption in the upper income brackets. This will tend to give an upward bias to our estimates of future demand as a function of rising incomes.

As for methodology, it is important to point out that even accurate cross-section data are not necessarily a reliable guide to future consumer behavior in response to rising average incomes. For example, rapid industrialization may bring about a change in the occupational pattern in the cities. A rising proportion of workers engaged in construction and similar heavy work could increase nutritional requirements and the pro-

17. See chapter 6, footnote 1. There are reasons for believing, however, that a rise in real food prices can be avoided (see chapter 8).

18. Reutlinger came to similar conclusions. He starts out from the premise, based on the National Sample Survey for 1971–72, that 276 million Indians (47 percent of the population) are below the 2,110 calorie level. With high income growth (2.6 percent per capita) that number would fall to 87 million (9 percent) by 1995; with low income growth (1.3 percent), 243 million (25 percent) would still be undernourished. A 1 percent annual rise in real food prices, however, would leave 21 percent of the population undernourished under the high-growth assumption and 37 percent under the low-growth assumption. Reutlinger estimates the present total calorie deficit at 7.5 percent of total food consumption. Based on our estimates in table 7-11, this would be equivalent to 11 million tons (the quantity of grain it would take to bring the undernourished population up to the 2,110 calorie level). By 1995, the calorie deficit would decline to 0.9 percent of total consumption under the high-growth assumption, and to 2.9 percent under the low-growth assumption. Without any redistributive measures, however, it would take thirty years to completely eliminate hunger under the high-growth assumption, and sixty years under the low-growth assumption. Reutlinger's income growth projections are similar to ours, but he projects a higher rate of population growth (2.3 percent compared with 2 percent). His consumption estimates require a 3.4 percent annual growth in food supply under the high-growth assumption, and 2.9 percent under the low-growth assumption (compare our estimates for 1975–2000 of 3.3 percent and 2.4 percent; for 1975–1990, of 3.2 percent and 2.3 percent). See Shlomo Reutlinger, "Malnutrition and Low Levels of Food Consumption: Current and Projected Magnitude of Problem in Selected Countries," draft working paper, World Bank, September 13, 1978.

portion of foodgrains in the urban diet compared with the present pattern at comparable income levels.

Experience shows, on the other hand, that the availability of a wider variety of foods in the course of a country's development may change the dietary pattern. This will generally result in a shift away from starchy foods to other foods. It is not unlikely, for example, that the development of efficient dairy and poultry industries close to urban areas will result in higher levels of consumption of livestock products than those projected here on the basis of present consumption patterns at the projected income levels. Since 80–85 percent of the food energy fed to livestock is lost in the conversion to milk, poultry, and eggs, this would result in a diet of higher quality but one providing fewer calories than the projected 3,400 calories per day.

CHAPTER EIGHT

Meeting the Food Demand from Domestic Production

THE PROBABLE DEMAND for food in 1990 and 2000 having been estimated, the question now is whether and how the demand could be met from domestic production. How much of the required additional output is likely to come from an expansion of the cropped area, from double cropping made possible by increased irrigation, from increased yields made possible by irrigation, increased fertilizer use, and increased use of high-yielding varieties?

The main steps in projecting output are as follows. First, an estimate is made of the likely increase in net sown and net irrigated areas under all crops. Second, estimates of gross irrigated and gross sown areas are derived on the basis of assumptions regarding double cropping. Then the proportion of this area that will be devoted to foodgrains and to other crops is estimated. The total output in 1990 and 2000 is projected after taking into consideration the probable effect on yields of irrigation, HYVs, increased use of fertilizers, and associated improvements in cultivating practices. Finally, the implications for production costs of the projected levels of irrigation and fertilizer use are considered.

Land and Water Resources

Table 8-1 shows the pattern of land utilization in India for the period 1950–51 to 1975–76. Between 1950–51 and 1955–56 the net sown area increased by 1.7 percent annually. Since then the annual rate of increase has slowed down from 0.5 percent in the decade 1955–56 to 1965–66 to 0.4 percent in the following decade. The scope for further increases in

Table 8-1. *Land Utilization, India, Selected Years, 1950–51 to 1975–76*
Millions of hectares

Classification	1950–51	1955–56	1960–61	1965–66	1970–71	1975–76[a]
Total uncultivated area	137.4	138.6	142.5	147.0	143.6	139.4
Forest	40.5	51.3	54.1	61.6	63.9	65.2
Not suitable for cultivation	47.5	48.4	50.8	49.5	44.6	42.1
Cultivable waste[b]	49.4	38.9	37.6	35.9	35.1	32.1
Total fallow area	28.1	24.1	22.8	22.4	19.4	19.0
Net sown area	118.7	129.2	133.2	136.2	140.7	142.2
Annual rate of increase, net sown area (percent)	1.7	0.6	0.4	0.7	0.2	

Source: 1950–71, Government of India, Ministry of Agriculture and Irrigation, Directorate of Economics and Statistics, *Indian Agriculture in Brief*, 16th ed. (Delhi: Controller of Publications, 1978); table 2.7, pp. 36–37; 1975–76, unpublished data, Ministry of Agriculture and Irrigation, Directorate of Economics and Statistics.
a. Preliminary
b. Includes permanent pastures and grazing land, land under miscellaneous tree crops, and other uncultivated land not included in fallow land.

the net sown area appears to be limited. The area under fallow land at the end of 1975–76 was only 19 million hectares, or 13 percent of the net sown area. About half the land in the category of cultivable waste is under permanent pastures and miscellaneous tree crops and the other half, which is either left fallow over the years or covered with shrubs, is probably not very economical to reclaim. Our projections call for a modest 8 million hectare increase between 1975 and 1990 (0.4 percent increase per year) and a subsequent decline to about the 1975 level of cultivation (see table 8-4).

Irrigation and improved water management, on the other hand, have been and will continue to be crucial to agricultural development in India. It was the development of irrigation since pre-independence days which made the green revolution possible. Further advances in double cropping and average yield require a substantial increase in water supplies and in the efficiency of water use.

India clearly has the potential to double or triple water supplies to agriculture. In 1972 the Indian Irrigation Commission estimated the ultimate irrigation potential at 81.7 gross irrigated hectares, as compared with 43 million in 1975–76. The relative contribution of surface and groundwater irrigation was put at 59.5 and 22.2 million hectares, respectively.[1] Subsequently, the figures have been revised upward to 107 million hectares (93.5 million hectare-meters—67 million of surface water and 26.5 million of groundwater). Major and medium-size projects (largely public systems) could be more than tripled, from 17.3 million hectares to 57 million; minor irrigation (small surface water diversion and storage projects and groundwater development) could be doubled, from 25.2 million to 50 million hectares. The estimated groundwater potential (26.5 million hectare-meters) is consistent with the estimated annual contribution of rainfall to groundwater reserves (about 37 million hectare-meters).[2]

In addition, a significant potential exists for induced groundwater

1. Government of India, Ministry of Irrigation and Power, *Report of the Irrigation Commission, 1972*, vol. 1 (Faridabad, Haryana, India: Thomson Press [India] Ltd., for Ministry of Irrigation and Power, 1972), p. 219. Average depth of irrigation, 0.87 meter.

2. Government of India, Planning Commission, *Draft Fifth Five Year Plan, 1974–79*, vol. 2 (Delhi: Controller of Publications, 1974), p. 105. Gross irrigated area for 1975 estimated from net irrigated area, assuming the same cropping ratio (125 percent) for major and minor irrigation as in 1974. A hectare-meter represents the water required to cover one hectare to the depth of one meter.

recharge in the Ganges basin. About one-half of the total river flow is lost to the system annually through excess river flows during the monsoon period. A significant portion of this could be captured by inducing ground-water recharge through the use of bunding, water spreading, and artificial lowering of the groundwater table in the dry season. It is estimated that an additional 6 million hectare-meters of water could be captured in this way.[3]

While the potential for expansion exists, there are limits on the speed with which India's water resources can be developed. Major and medium-size irrigation projects, in particular, require enormous investments and long lead times. To get a rough idea of possible rates of expansion, it is useful to review the record of the past twenty-five years (table 8-2). In that period, the total net irrigated area increased by 65 percent, from 20.9 million to 34.5 million hectares. Slightly over 40 percent of that expansion (5.6 million hectares) is attributable to major public (canal) irrigation systems; the remainder (8 million hectares) to minor irrigation. The average annual rate of growth over the entire period was about 2 percent. The green revolution brought a sharp increase, to 3.4 percent, in the annual rate of growth of the net irrigated area between 1965–66 and 1970–71. The growth rate slowed down to 2.1 percent between 1970–71 and 1975–76 but appears to have recovered to about 3 percent in 1975–76 to 1977–78.[4]

For the period up to 1990, the net irrigated area can be expected to increase at about the long-term average annual rate (1.8 percent). Most of the increase will come from the completion of major and medium-size irrigation projects now underway. After 1990, we expect the rate of expansion to accelerate to 2.3 percent, to give an overall annual growth rate of 2 percent for the period 1975 to 2000 (table 8-4). Much of that expansion should come from groundwater development in the alluvial areas of northeastern India, which has been neglected in the past because of the generally favorable rainfall there. The outlook has now been changed by the more exacting water requirements of the high-yielding varieties, and

3. Roger Revelle and V. Lakshminarayama, "The Ganges Water Machine," *Science,* vol. 188 (May 9, 1975), pp. 611–16. An even more ambitious scheme, the "Garland Canal," involving linking the major river systems, would make large-scale transfers of water from the Brahmaputra and Ganges to dry areas in central and southern India. See *Hindu* (Madras), March 30, 1979, and *Times of India* (New Delhi), April 4, 1979.

4. Government of India, Planning Commission, *Draft Five Year Plan, 1978–83* (Delhi: Controller of Publications, 1978), p. 135.

Table 8-2. Net Irrigated Area, by Source, India, Selected Years, 1950–51 to 1975–76
Millions of hectares

Source and rate of increase	1950–51	1955–56	1960–61	1965–66	1970–71	1975–76
Major and medium-size projects[a]	8.3	9.4	10.4	11.0	12.8	13.9
Annual rate of increase (percent)		2.5	2.0	1.1	3.0	1.6
Minor projects[b]	12.6	13.4	14.3	15.4	18.3	20.6
Annual rate of increase (percent)		1.2	1.3	1.5	3.5	2.4
Total	20.9	22.8	24.7	26.3	31.1	34.5
Annual rate of increase (percent)		1.7	1.6	1.3	3.4	2.1

Source: 1950–71, Government of India, Ministry of Agriculture and Irrigation, Directorate of Economics and Statistics, Directorate of Economics and Statistics, *Indian Agriculture in Brief*, 16th ed. (Delhi: Controller of Publications, 1978), table 2.8, pp. 38–39; 1975–76, unpublished data, Ministry of Agriculture and Irrigation, Directorate of Economics and Statistics. Data for 1975–76 are preliminary. Figures are rounded.

a. Irrigation by canals.

b. Irrigation by tubewells, tanks, and other methods.

the realization of the possibilities of multiple cropping based on the underground storage of excess river flows during the monsoon period.

In most regions of India, irrigation is a prerequisite for growing more than one crop a year. As can be seen from table 8-3, the cropping intensity is greater on irrigated land.[5] The importance of irrigation as a factor facilitating double cropping was enhanced by the introduction of fast-maturing HYVs. Further increases in cropping intensity will depend largely on the expansion of the irrigated area.

Table 8-3. *Cropping Intensity Indexes,*[a] *India, Selected Years, 1950–51 to 1975–76*

Year	Irrigated area[b]	Other area	Total
1950–51	108	112	111
1955–56	113	114	114
1960–61	113	115	115
1965–66	117	113	114
1970–71.	123	116	118
1975–76[e]	124	119	120

Source: Government of India, Ministry of Agriculture and Irrigation, Directorate of Economics and Statistics, *Estimates of Area and Production of Principal Crops in India, 1977–78* (Delhi: Controller of Publications, 1979), app. I, p. 145.
a. The ratio of gross cropped area to net cropped area, times 100.
b. See footnote 5 to this chapter.
c. Preliminary figures.

Between 1965–66 and 1975–76, the cropping intensity on irrigated land rose from 117 to 124, or at a rate of 0.6 percent per year; in Punjab and Haryana it is already at 146. We have accordingly projected the cropping intensity on irrigated land from 124 in 1975 to 146 in 1990 and 165 in the year 2000, implying an annual rate of increase of slightly over 1 percent. The resulting gross irrigated area is found by multiplying the net irrigated area by the cropping intensity (table 8-4). The projected expansion of the gross irrigated area from 43 million hectares in 1975 to 94 million hectares by 2000 is an annual increase of 3.1 percent.

Improvements in water management are likely to play a much greater role than in the past in supplementing the benefits of further expansion of the net irrigated area. As mentioned earlier (see chapter 3), the public water system in India is thinly spread and often poorly maintained. Its

5. The cropping intensity (multiple cropping index) is the ratio of gross cropped area to net cropped area, times 100. It should be noted that table 8-3 understates the amount of double cropping made possible by irrigation because land which is irrigated only in one season (usually the dry season) is not counted as double-cropped irrigated land.

Table 8-4. *Net and Gross Sown and Irrigated Areas, India, 1975, and Projections for 1990 and 2000*
Area in millions of hectares

Item	1975ᵃ	1990	2000
Irrigated area			
Net area	34.5	45.3	57.0
Cropping intensity indexᵇ	124	146	165
Gross area	42.9	66.1	94.0
Unirrigated area			
Net area	107.7	104.7	87.0
Cropping intensity indexᵇ	119	121	125
Gross area	128.1	126.7	108.8
Total sown area			
Total net sown area	142.2	150.0	144.0
Cropping intensity indexᵇ	120	129	141
Total gross sown area	171.0	192.8	202.8

Source: 1975, same as table 8-3; 1990 and 2000, authors' projections.
a. Preliminary figures.
b. The ratio of gross cropped area to net cropped area, times 100.

delivery capacity is highly variable from month to month and from year to year, depending on rainfall and river flows. Seepage and evaporation losses in channels as well as in the field and poor seasonal distribution greatly reduce its efficiency, by as much as one-third to one-half, compared with standards achieved in the United States. Some damage is caused, furthermore, by flooding and by poor drainage resulting in excess salinity. It has been estimated that about 50 percent of the irrigated area in the country is in need of improvement.[6]

In contrast to the anticipated expansion of the irrigated area, we expect that the net unirrigated area will decline from 107.7 million hectares in 1975 to 104.7 million in 1990 and 87.0 million in the year 2000. Until 1990, this decline will be approximately offset by the expected increase in multiple cropping; after 1990, we project a decline in the gross unirrigated area (table 8-4).

Table 8-4 summarizes the projections of net sown area, broken down into irrigated and unirrigated areas, the relevant cropping intensities, and the resulting gross sown areas. The total gross sown area shows a projected annual rate of increase of 0.6 percent from 1975 to 2000, mainly because of the increase in double cropping in areas under irrigation.

6. United Nations, Economic and Social Council, Committee on Natural Resources, *Water for Agriculture,* E/C.7/L.54, December 8, 1976, p. 5.

Output

In what follows, output is projected separately for foodgrains, other food crops, and nonfood crops.

Foodgrains

Our demand projections for foodgrains show an annual growth rate of 2.7 percent between 1975 and 1990, slowing down to 2.4 percent in the following decade (table 7-7). Given the projected increase in average yields of foodgrains (table 8-7), we estimate that the required increase in production can be achieved with only small additions to total sown area (5 million hectares between 1975 and 1990). In the following decade we project a reduction of 16 million hectares in the gross area sown to foodgrains (table 8-5). The share of foodgrains in total sown area is expected to decline from 75 percent in 1975 to 58 percent in 2000. The gross irrigated area under foodgrains is projected to double between 1975 and 2000; however, its share of the total irrigated area will decline in that period from 80 to 76 percent.

Table 8-5. *Gross Sown and Irrigated Areas, All Foodgrains, India, 1975, and Projections for 1990 and 2000*

Year	Gross sown area		Gross irrigated area	
	Amount (millions of hectares)	Percent of total gross sown area	Amount (millions of hectares)	Percent of total gross irrigated area
1975[a]	128.2	75	34.1	80
1990	133.0	69	52.0	79
2000	116.7	58	71.0	76

Source: 1975, same as table 8-3, table 1, p. 9; app. I, p. 147; 1990 and 2000, authors' projections.
a. Preliminary figures.

Table 8-6 shows how the total sown and irrigated areas may be allocated among individual foodgrains. Between 1975 and 2000, the areas sown to rice, wheat, and pulses are projected to increase, while those under coarse grains will decline rapidly. The underlying assumption is that with increases in per capita income, consumer demand will shift to the preferred grains (rice, wheat, and pulses), which show a higher income elasticity of demand.

By the turn of the century, we expect roughly 60 percent of the total foodgrain area, as against 27 percent in 1975, to be under irrigation. All

Table 8-6. Gross Sown and Irrigated Areas, by Foodgrain, India, 1975, and Projections for 1990 and 2000
Millions of hectares

Crop	Total sown area			Irrigated area			Unirrigated area		
	1975	1990	2000	1975[a]	1990	2000	1975	1990	2000
Rice	39.5	43.5	44.0	15.1	25.2	35.4	24.4	18.3	8.6
Wheat	20.4	24.7	25.0	12.6	19.0	25.0	7.8	5.7	0
Coarse grains	43.8	38.8	20.0	4.3	3.6	3.5	39.5	35.2	16.5
Pulses	24.5	26.0	27.7	2.0	4.2	7.1	22.5	21.8	20.6
All foodgrains	128.2	133.0	116.7	34.1	52.0	71.0	94.1	81.0	45.7

Source: 1975, same as table 8-3, table 1, pp. 2–9; app. I, pp. 146–47; 1990 and 2000, authors' projections.
a. Preliminary figures.

of the wheat and 80 percent of the rice will be grown on irrigated land. Coarse grains and pulses will be grown mainly on unirrigated land.

The projected yields of foodgrains are shown in table 8-7. Yields on the irrigated area are expected to increase at an annual rate of about 2 percent between 1975 and 2000; those on the unirrigated area at less than 1 percent. However, because of the increasing proportion of the irrigated area in the total, average yields on the total gross sown area will increase by 2.8 percent a year. This rate of growth may be compared with an average of 1.9 percent achieved in the past quarter century and a growth rate of 2.8 percent in weather-adjusted yields (for all cereals) in the period 1966–67 to 1977–78.

Table 8-7. *Average Yields of Foodgrains on Irrigated and Unirrigated Land, India, 1975, and Projections for 1990 and 2000*
Kilograms per hectare

	Crop				
Item and year	Rice	Wheat	Coarse grains	Pulses	All foodgrains
All land					
1975	1,246	1,409	684	533	943
1990	1,744	1,904	809	731	1,303
2000	2,451	2,700	898	928	1,889
Irrigated land					
1975[a]	1,600	1,600	1,300	900	1,525
1990	2,100	2,100	1,800	1,150	2,009
2000	2,700	2,700	2,000	1,300	2,525
Unirrigated land					
1975	988	1,105	625	496	723
1990	1,253	1,250	708	650	850
2000	1,427	...	750	800	900

Sources: All land, 1975, Ministry of Agriculture and Irrigation, *Estimates of Area and Production of Principal Crops in India, 1977–78.* Irrigated averages, 1975, calculated from data on states in ibid.; unirrigated yields were calculated as residuals. Figures for 1990 and 2000, authors' projections.

a. Preliminary figures.

This increase in the yields of irrigated grains is assumed to come mainly from two measurable sources: increased plantings of high-yielding varieties, and greater use of fertilizers (see table 8-8).[7] By the year 2000, the entire irrigated area under rice, wheat, and coarse grains is expected to be

7. No explicit allowance is made here for intangible factors such as improved cultivating practices and greater efficiency of water use.

Table 8-8. *Factors Affecting Yields of Irrigated Foodgrains, India, 1975, and Projections for 1990 and 2000*

Crop	Percent of area under HYVs			Average fertilizer dose (kilograms per hectare)[a]		
	1975	1990	2000	1975	1990	2000
Rice	74.4	90.0	100.0	55	105	170
Wheat	100.0	100.0	100.0	55	105	170
Coarse grains	100.0	100.0	100.0	30	84	111
Pulses	...	...	...	20	50	75
All foodgrains	82.3	87.1	90.0	50	99	158

Sources: 1975, derived from Fertilizer Association of India, *Fertilizer Statistics, 1976–77*, pp. II-81–II-83; data on irrigated area from Ministry of Agriculture and Irrigation, *Estimates of Area and Production of Principal Crops in India, 1977–78*, app. I, pp. 146–47; 1990 and 2000, authors' projections.

a. Average fertilizer dosages have been calculated as follows. The base yield of irrigated grains (without fertilizer) is assumed to be 1 ton per hectare for wheat, rice, and coarse grains, and 0.7 ton per hectare for pulses. Average response ratios for 1975 are assumed to be 11:1 for wheat and rice, and 10:1 for coarse grains and pulses; for 1990 and 2000 average response ratios are projected to decline to 10.5:1 and 10:1 for wheat and rice, 9.5:1 and 9:1 for coarse grains, and 9:1 and 8:1 for pulses. See "Evaluation of Yardsticks of Additional Production for the Use of Fertilizers on High-Yielding and Locally Improved Tall Varieties of Cereals" (New Delhi: Indian Council of Agriculture Research, Institute of Agricultural Research Statistics, 1973).

planted in HYVs. It is assumed that certified seeds will be available in adequate quantities, and that new high-yielding varieties will be developed continuously so that existing varieties can be replaced before they begin to degenerate. No HYVs of pulses exist at present; we assume none will be developed in the future.

Average fertilizer dosages on irrigated foodgrains are projected to triple between 1975 and 2000, from 50 kilograms per hectare in 1975 to 158 kilograms per hectare in 2000. The fertilizer dosages have been estimated on the basis of an average response ratio in the range of 10:1 over a base yield (without fertilizer) of 1 ton per hectare. Yields of unirrigated foodgrains are expected to rise much more slowly for two reasons. First, by the year 2000, the unirrigated areas will consist mainly of coarse grains and pulses (see table 8-6) whose average yields are low compared to those of wheat and rice. Second, the future scope for accelerated growth in yields of these crops is limited by low fertilizer response ratios and the absence of improved varieties that can be grown under rainfed conditions. Future growth in yields will come mainly from two sources: improvements in cultivation practices, and increased use of fertilizer (table 8-9).

A summary table showing total projected output (which is the same as the projected demand for foodgrains) and the input requirements for achieving that output are shown in table 8-10.

Table 8-9. *Fertilizer Dosages for Unirrigated Foodgrains, India, 1975, and Projections for 1990 and 2000*
Kilograms per hectare

Crop	Average fertilizer dose		
	1975	1990	2000
Rice	11.0	40.4	59.8
Wheat	6.0	22.1	...
Coarse grains	3.0	14.8	20.8
Pulses	0.5	22.5	43.9
All foodgrains	4.6	23.2	38.5

Source: 1975, estimated using the data given in National Council of Applied Economic Research, *Fertilizer Use on Selected Crops in India* (New Delhi: NCAER and the Fertilizer Association of India, 1974), adjusted upward to take account of increased overall fertilizer use in 1975; 1990 and 2000, authors' projections, estimated on the basis of response ratios of approximately 7:1.

Table 8-10. *Total Output of Foodgrains and Input Requirements, India, 1975, and Projections for 1990 and 2000*

Item	1975	1990	2000
Total output (millions of metric tons)	121.0	173.3	220.5
Input requirements			
Sown area (millions of hectares)	128.2	133.0	116.7
Irrigated area (millions of hectares)	34.1[a]	52.0	71.0
Area under HYVs (millions of hectares)	32.1[a]	47.8	63.9
Fertilizer use (millions of metric tons)	2.2	7.0	13.0

Source: Same as table 8-5; and Fertilizer Association of India, *Fertilizer Statistics, 1976–77*, pp. I-83–I-84, II-83.
a. Preliminary figures.

Other Food Crops

Food crops other than foodgrains consist, in the main, of sugarcane, oilseeds, and fruits and vegetables. The total demand for these crops, in grain equivalents, is projected to grow from an estimated 30.6 million metric tons in 1975 to 112.2 million metric tons in the year 2000 (see table 7-8). It is assumed that the relative importance of the three main types of other food crops will continue to be the same as in 1970. Thus, in terms of calorie or grain equivalents, roughly 45 percent of the total demand for other food crops is assumed to be for sugarcane, 30 percent for oilseeds, and 25 percent for fruits and vegetables.[8]

8. Relative importance based on table 1-1. Roots are included as vegetables.

In estimating output we have proceeded as follows. First, the base-period production of sugarcane, oilseeds, and fruits and vegetables was converted to grain equivalents by using the conversion ratios shown in the FAO commodity projections.[9] Area in hectares and production and average yields in grain equivalents for 1975 are shown in table 8-11.

Table 8-11. *Area, Production, and Yields of Other Food Crops, India, 1975*

Crop	Area (millions of hectares)	Production (millions of metric tons, grain equivalent)[a]	Yield (kilograms per hectare, grain equivalent)[a]
Sugarcane	2.76	14.41	5,218
Oilseeds	15.22	9.91	651
Fruits and vegetables	3.96	6.20	1,566
Total, other food crops	21.94	30.52	1,391

Source: Based on data from Government of India, Ministry of Agriculture and Irrigation, Directorate of Economics and Statistics.

a. Grain equivalents were estimated by using the following conversion factors: 1 metric ton of grain = 1 metric ton of oilseeds, 10 metric tons of sugarcane, 12.5 metric tons of fruits and vegetables, 5 metric tons of potatoes, and 3.33 metric tons of root crops (sweet potatoes and tapioca).

Second, in projecting average yields of sugarcane and oilseeds we adopted an average growth rate of 1.3 percent for the period 1975–90 and 1.5 percent for 1990–2000. These rates represent the middle of the range between the 1 percent average annual growth rate observed for both sugarcane and oilseeds in the period 1960–75 and estimates based on the report of the National Commission on Agriculture,[10] which imply an average annual increase between 1975 and 2000 of 1.8 percent for sugarcane and 1.9 percent for oilseeds (figures which we believe to be too optimistic). For fruits and vegetables, we have assumed very moderate increases in average yields between 1975 and 2000. The projected yields in grain equivalents are shown in table 8-12.

Third, projections of irrigated area and fertilizer use, the two major determinants of yield, were made as follows. Between 1960 and 1975, the proportion of irrigated area to total area under the crop increased from 3.3 percent to 7.9 percent (6.0 percent annual increase) for oilseeds, and from 69 to 77 percent (0.7 percent per year) for sugarcane.

9. Food and Agriculture Organization of the United Nations, *Agricultural Commodity Projections, 1970–1980*, vol. 2 (Rome: FAO, 1971), p. 32.

10. See *Report of the National Commission on Agriculture, 1976*, pt. 6: *Crop Production, Sericulture and Apiculture*, Government of India, Ministry of Agriculture and Irrigation (Delhi: Controller of Publications, 1976), p. 252.

Table 8-12. *Yields of Other Food Crops, India, 1975, and Projections for 1990 and 2000*
Kilograms per hectare, grain equivalent[a]

Crop	1975	1990	2000
Sugarcane	5,218	6,399	7,426
Oilseeds	651	776	900
Fruits and vegetables	1,566	1,600	1,650
Total, other food crops	1,391	1,666	1,868

Source: 1975, same as table 8-11; 1990 and 2000, authors' projections.
a. See table 8-11, note a.

The ratio of irrigated area to total cropped area under sugarcane and oilseeds is projected to increase at the same rate as in the past. It is assumed that fruits and vegetables will continue to be grown under rainfed conditions.

Data on fertilizer use are available for individual crops only for 1970 from the NCAER study.[11] They show that out of the total quantity of NPK[12] used, 18 percent went to sugarcane, 4 percent to oilseeds, and none to fruits and vegetables. Using this as the basis, we calculated 1975 average dosages for sugarcane and oilseeds in the same way as for wheat and rice, obtaining 186 kilograms per hectare of NPK for sugarcane and 6.6 kilograms per hectare for oilseeds. Future requirements are calculated on the basis of average response ratios of 15:1 for sugarcane and 5:1 for oilseeds.

The resulting projections of irrigated area and fertilizer use are shown in table 8-13.

Fourth, the area that will be required, given the projected yields, to meet the projected demand for other food crops is shown in table 8-14. And finally, total output and a summary of input requirements are shown in table 8-15.

Industrial and Other Crops

For these nonfood crops only land and fertilizer requirements have been projected. For cotton, which is the main crop in this group, accounting for about half the acreage, we have based our projections on the

11. National Council of Applied Economic Research, *Fertilizer Use on Selected Crops in India* (New Delhi: NCAER and the Fertilizer Association of India, 1974).
12. Fertilizer expressed in pure nutrients of nitrogen, phosphorus, and potassium (NPK).

Table 8-13. *Irrigated Area and Fertilizer Consumption, Other Food Crops, India, 1975, and Projections for 1990 and 2000*

Crop	Irrigated area (millions of hectares)			Average fertilizer dosage (kilograms per hectare)		
	1975[a]	1990	2000	1975[a]	1990	2000
Sugarcane	2.23	3.66	6.23	186.00	261.00	329.00
Oilseeds	1.20	4.25	9.17	6.60	34.00	59.00
Fruits and vegetables	0.00	0.00	0.00	0.00	0.00	0.00
Total, other food crops	3.43	7.91	15.40	28.32	51.08	71.53

Sources: 1975, same as table 8-3, app. I, p. 146; NCAER, *Fertilizer Use on Selected Crops in India*; 1990 and 2000, authors' projections.
a. Preliminary figures.

Table 8-14. *Area under Other Food Crops, India, 1975, and Projections for 1990 and 2000*
Millions of hectares

Crop	1975	1990	2000
Sugarcane	2.76	4.31	6.80
Oilseeds	15.22	22.16	34.90
Fruits and vegetables	3.96	10.31	18.36
Total, other food crops	21.94	36.78	60.06

Sources: 1975, same as table 8-11; 1990 and 2000, authors' projections.

Table 8-15. *Total Output of Other Food Crops and Input Requirements, India, 1975, and Projections for 1990 and 2000*

Item	1975	1990	2000
Total output (millions of metric tons, grain equivalent)	30.5	61.3	112.2
Input requirements			
Sown area (millions of hectares)	21.14	36.78	60.06
Irrigated area (millions of hectares)	3.34	7.91	15.40
Fertilizer consumption (millions of metric tons)	0.62	1.88	4.30

Source: For 1975, output and sown area, same as table 8-11; irrigated area, same as table 8-13; fertilizer consumption calculated as average dosage (from table 8-13) times sown area; 1990 and 2000, authors' projections.

demand projections by the National Commission on Agriculture. The commission expects total demand for cotton to almost triple, from 1.0 million tons in 1975 to 2.9 million tons in 2000.[13] We have further assumed that this demand will be met by an increase in yields from 139 kilograms per hectare in 1975 to 205 kilograms in 2000 (based on the trend rate of 1.57 percent per year observed in 1960–75), and an increase in area from 7.4 million to 14.1 million hectares. The irrigated area under cotton is projected to increase from 1.6 million hectares in 1975 to 4.5 million hectares in 2000; the basis for this projection is the same as for sugar and oilseeds.[14] Fertilizer use in 1975 has been estimated in the same way as for wheat and other crops;[15] the average dose comes to about 25 kilograms per hectare. Future dosages have been calculated on the basis of a 6:1 response ratio.

A similar procedure has been followed for jute and mesta, tobacco, tea, and coffee, which together account for another 2 million hectares. For the remainder of this group we have assumed a slight decline in land and fertilizer requirements. The resulting input projections are summarized in table 8-16.

Table 8-16. *Summary of Input Requirements for Industrial and Other Nonfood Crops, India, 1975, and Projections for 1990 and 2000*

Item	1975	1990	2000
Total sown area (millions of hectares)	19.0	23.0	26.0
Irrigated area (millions of hectares)	4.7	6.2	7.6
Average fertilizer dosage (kilograms per hectare)	10.5	15.2	19.2
Fertilizer requirements (millions of metric tons)	0.20	0.35	0.50

Source: Authors' calculations, based on *Report of the National Commission on Agriculture*, pt. 3: *Demand and Supply*, Government of India, Ministry of Agriculture and Irrigation (Delhi: Controller of Publications, 1976).

Implications for Production Costs

There is a widely held view that further increases in food production to meet the rising demand of a rapidly growing population, while tech-

13. *Report of the National Commission on Agriculture*, pt. 3: *Demand and Supply* (Delhi: Controller of Publications, 1976), table 10.9, p. 23.
14. See chapter 7.
15. See chapter 2.

nically possible, will inevitably be far more costly than in the past.[16] The massive investments that are required for irrigation, energy, and fertilizer production (see chapter 9), the rising costs of irrigation as the most economical groundwater and storage sites are exhausted, and diminishing returns from additional applications of land, water, and fertilizer are usually cited in support of this thesis.

Plausible as it may seem, the thesis is not supported by experience. In the United States, for example, real prices of basic crops have shown a declining trend over the past quarter century as agricultural productivity[17] increased more rapidly than productivity in the rest of the economy. Evidently, the effect of diminishing returns was more than offset by the cost-reducing effects of factor substitution, improved cultivation practices, and technological advances such as hybrid seeds.

For India, which is in the early stages of its agricultural revolution, the potential gains are even greater. First, applications of water and fertilizer are far short of the economic optimum, even at the present level of technology. This means that increased use of these inputs may be expected to yield returns, at current prices, that will more than pay for the cost of the inputs. For instance, average fertilizer use on irrigated foodgrains is still only fifty kilograms per hectare; the available evidence suggests that the dosage could be doubled without any noticeable decline in marginal returns from fertilizers. Second, the scope for increasing efficiency as a result of the use of inputs is much greater in India. Finally, there is no reason to believe that scientists have reached the end of the road in genetics and other cost-reducing technology.

Here we consider only the first aspect, which lends itself best to quantitative analysis: given present technology, can we expect the projected increase in inputs to pay off in terms of additional output, without an increase in real prices? The inputs we have singled out are irrigation and fertilizer. Pesticides have been ignored because they are a relatively small component of production costs. Labor costs can be neglected because the existing manpower is now woefully underemployed: unit labor costs may be expected to decline as production increases. Machinery is not expected to become a major element of agricultural production costs for some time to come. Improvements in rural infrastructure are necessary, but the portion of these costs that could be considered chargeable to agri-

16. See, for example, Lester R. Brown, *By Bread Alone* (Praeger for the Overseas Development Council, 1974), pp. 13–14.

17. Farm output per unit of input.

cultural production is difficult to determine and would not, in any event, represent a major cost-raising factor.

Irrigation

The annual costs of irrigation per hectare[18] consist of two main elements: capital costs (amortization plus interest) and operating and maintenance costs (including energy costs to operate the pumps). Capital costs vary widely: they tend to be highest for major irrigation projects involving high dams and long-distance canals, and much less for the improvement of existing systems and for tubewells and minor irrigation projects such as small river diversion canals, or ponds. For major dams, investment costs must be allocated between electric power generation and irrigation—a difficult problem since government-controlled power and water rates do not necessarily reflect the relative economic values in a free market.

In the calculations which follow (table 8-17), the estimates of investment costs, based on a number of sources, were converted to annual costs on the basis of a straight-line amortization of 2 percent for major irrigation projects (fifty years), 3.3 percent for improvements of existing systems (thirty years), and 6.7 percent for minor irrigation projects (fifteen years). The real interest rate is assumed to be 7 percent. Maintenance and operating costs are based on a number of sources predating the increase in the prices of basic fuels in 1974. To allow for the effects of that increase on energy prices at the farm level, we have adjusted pre-1974 energy costs upward by 100 percent.

Estimates based on the Planning Commission's Fifth Plan document place average investment costs for major and medium-size irrigation projects during 1968–69 to 1973–74 at about $450 per gross irrigated hectare. During the period of the Fifth Plan, per hectare costs rose to about $750.[19] By now they are probably about $900, in 1975 prices.[20] We assume that by the end of the century the cost of major and medium-size irrigation projects per gross hectare will rise to $1,350, in 1975 prices.

18. Following Indian practice, we take the average depth of irrigation to be three feet, which is representative of the average amount of water required for a crop of cereals. (Water requirements are less for wheat, greater for rice.)

19. Authors' calculations, 1975 U.S. dollars. See Government of India, Planning Commission, *Draft Fifth Five Year Plan, 1974–79* (Delhi: Controller of Publications, 1974), vol. 2, p. 106; and *Draft Five Year Plan, 1978–83* (1978), p. 135.

20. M. S. Swaminathan, "Indian Agriculture at the Crossroads," *Indian Journal of Agricultural Economics,* vol. 32 (October–December 1977), p. 18.

Table 8-17. *Estimated Costs of Irrigation, India, 1975–2000*
1975 U.S. dollars per gross hectare

	Ranges for 1975–2000		
Type of cost	Major irrigation	Improvement of existing systems	Minor irrigation[a]
Investment costs	900–1,350	200–400	350–450
Annual costs	77–115	20–40	102–167
Amortization	18–27[b]	6–14[c]	23–30[d]
Interest[e]	32–47	8–14	13–17
Operation and maintenance	27–41[f]	6–12[f]	16–20
Fuel and power	. . .	. . .	50–100[g]

Sources: Authors' calculations, based on Government of India, Planning Commission, *Draft Five Year Plan, 1978–83* (Delhi: Controller of Publications, 1978), pp. 134–39; Food and Agriculture Organization of the United Nations, *Indicative World Plan for Agricultural Development to 1975 and 1985,* Provisional Regional Study 4: *Asia and the Far East,* vol. 1 (Rome: FAO, 1968). See table 9-6 for detailed investment cost estimates.
a. Mainly tubewells.
b. 2 percent (fifty years).
c. 3.3 percent (thirty years).
d. 6.7 percent (fifteen years).
e. 7 percent on balance outstanding.
f. 3 percent of investment costs.
g. Assuming an average pumping depth of 40 feet.

If we assume an average life of fifty years, a real interest rate of 7 percent (on the balance outstanding), and operating and maintenance costs of 3 percent, the annual cost amounts to $77 per gross hectare in 1975, rising to $115 by the year 2000 (in 1975 dollars).

The costs of improving existing systems are highly variable, depending on the amount of work to be done (compacting water courses, repairing ditch banks and turnouts, lining canals, installing auxiliary tubewells to supplement surface water supplies when needed, drainage where required, and so forth). We have adopted here a range from $200 to $400.[21] Assuming a life of thirty years, a 7 percent interest rate, and operating and maintenance costs at 3 percent of the investment cost, total annual costs range between $20 and $40 per gross hectare.

For minor irrigation (mainly tubewells), investment costs are esti-

21. Estimates by FAO for Asia as a whole range from $300 to $700 per net irrigated hectare. See UN Economic and Social Council, Committee on Natural Resources, *Water for Agriculture.* The Trilateral Commission report on increasing rice production in South and Southeast Asia puts the cost at $400 per hectare (in 1975 constant prices) for the area as a whole. Umberto Colombo, D. Gale Johnson, and Toshio Shishido, *Reducing Malnutrition in Developing Countries: Increasing Rice Production in South and Southeast Asia,* Report of the Trilateral North-South Food Task Force to the Trilateral Commission (Trilateral Commission, 1978), p. 31.

mated at $350 to $450 per gross hectare.[22] With a life of fifteen years, interest at 7 percent, and operating and maintenance costs (excluding fuel and power) of $16 to $20 per gross hectare, annual costs other than energy costs are very low ($52 to $67). Annual costs of energy to operate a pump lifting water from a depth of 40 feet have varied between $25 and $50 per gross hectare (electricity being the cheapest energy source in most locations).[23] However, if it is assumed that energy costs will have doubled once the higher crude energy prices are fully reflected in electric power rates and retail prices of petroleum products, the annual cost per hectare of tubewell irrigation is likely to run higher than that of canal irrigation.

Fertilizer

World market prices for fertilizer have fallen from their peak in 1975 and have leveled off, in real terms, at somewhat higher levels than those prevailing before the energy crisis. In 1977, nitrogenous fertilizer was about 50 percent more expensive, in real terms, than in 1972; phosphatic fertilizer, 30 percent; and potash, 10 percent. It is assumed here that these higher price levels (reflecting higher costs of energy) will continue. We have assumed, further, that fertilizer will be available to Indian farmers at the prices paid by American farmers in 1977—$222, $320, and $154 per metric ton of pure nutrient content of anhydrous ammonia, concentrated superphosphate, and muriate of potash, respectively.[24] Assuming a 4:2:1 ratio of use, the weighted average price of a ton of NPK works out at $240, in 1975 dollars. The average fertilizer dose of 150 kilograms per gross irrigated hectare projected for 2000 will, therefore, cost $36.

Annual costs of irrigation and fertilizer combined will thus amount to between $113 and $203 per gross hectare.

Returns

To get a rough idea of the net benefit from irrigation and fertilizer, the value of production from unirrigated and unfertilized land must be deducted from the anticipated gross value of the product, and then the

22. Based on Government of India, Planning Commission, *Draft Five Year Plan, 1978–83.*

23. Based on a consensus of experts: Conference on the Economics of Irrigation, Tucson, Arizona, March 1–2, 1976, summary, p. 5.

24. In 1975 dollars. Based on data in U.S. Department of Agriculture, Economic Research Service, *1978 Fertilizer Situation* (USDA, December 1977), tables 5, 6.

resulting increase in the value of production compared with the annual costs per gross hectare of irrigation and fertilizer.

The average yield of wheat and rice without irrigation and fertilizer is assumed to be 0.5 ton per hectare. The incremental yield due to irrigation and fertilizer comes to 2.7 tons projected for 2000 (see table 8-7), less 0.5 ton without irrigation and fertilizer, for a net yield of 2.2 tons per hectare. The projected proportions of wheat and rice in total cereal production from irrigated land in 2000[25] mean that the additional 2.2 tons will consist of 0.9 ton of wheat and 1.3 tons of rice. When these quantities are valued at the (conservatively estimated) prospective world market prices, adjusted for transportation costs to India, of $120 for wheat and $220 for rice (in 1975 dollars), we obtain an incremental gross return, due to irrigation and fertilizer, of $394 per hectare. This is well in excess of the estimated annual cost of irrigation and fertilizer of $113 to $203 per hectare.

25. Area times yield from tables 8-6 and 8-7 gives 59 percent rice and 41 percent wheat.

CHAPTER NINE

Policy Implications

FOOD POLICY decisions are greatly influenced by national and international perceptions of future prospects regarding population and income growth and the possibilities of mobilizing resources for increased food production. This is as it should be. But public perceptions of the problem have changed a great deal as a result, in part, of events that proved to be transitory. Hence, policy prescriptions have varied almost as much as the underlying projections of supply and demand.

There is no foolproof way of deciding among different sets of projections. Policymakers must evaluate the basic assumptions, and they should not accept without question the demand and supply elasticities, input-output coefficients, and similar devices commonly used in such analyses. Projected growth rates need to be checked against past performance and the existing resource potential. Comparisons with other projections can be helpful in tracking down questionable assumptions or data. Above all, policymakers should be wary of long-term forecasts of import deficits ("food gaps"), particularly those based on simple extrapolations of short- or medium-term production trends.

Are Our Projections Realistic?

To provide a historical perspective, the growth rates projected here may be compared with the growth rates observed in 1950–75 and 1960–75 (table 9-1). Our projected growth rate for total food (calorie) demand (3.4 percent for the next twenty-five years) is about one-half of a percentage point higher than the corresponding rate in the past twenty-five years. It is probably on the high side. It reflects our expectation that the rate of population growth will decline only slightly and that income

Table 9-1. *Annual Growth Rates, India, 1950–75, and Projections for 1975–2000*
Percent

Item	1950–75ᵃ	1960–75ᵃ	1975–90	1990–2000	1975–2000
Population	2.2	2.2	2.0	1.9	2.0
Urban population (as percent of total)	1.0	1.3	2.1	3.1	2.5
Income per capita	1.3	1.2	3.0	4.4	3.5
Per capita foodgrain demandᵇ	0.4	0.2	0.7	0.3	0.5
Total foodgrain demandᵇ	2.6	2.4	2.7	2.2	2.5
Per capita demand for food (grain equivalent)	n.a.ᶜ	n.a.ᶜ	1.2	1.6	1.4
Total demand for food (grain equivalent)	n.a.ᶜ	n.a.ᶜ	3.2	3.5	3.3
Food production (grain equivalent)	n.a.ᶜ	n.a.ᶜ	3.2	3.5	3.4
Foodgrain production	2.8	2.8	2.4	2.4	2.4
Foodgrain yields	1.9	2.2ᵈ	2.2	3.7	2.8
Gross cropped area	1.0	0.7	0.9	0.5	0.7
Net cropped area	0.7	0.4	0.4	-0.4	0.0
Cropping intensity, total	0.3	0.3	0.5	0.9	0.6
Gross irrigated area	2.6	2.9	2.9	3.5	3.1
Net irrigated area	2.0	2.2	1.8	2.3	2.1
Cropping intensity, irrigated area	0.6	0.6	1.1	1.2	1.1
Fertilizer consumption	n.a.	16.5	7.4	6.6	7.1

Sources: Population, 1950–75, Population Division of the United Nations Secretariat; fertilizer consumption, 1960–75, Fertilizer Association of India, *Fertilizer Statistics, 1976–77,* and earlier issues; all other data, authors' calculations from tables 7-2, 7-3, 7-4, 7-7, 7-11, 8-3, 8-4, 8-7, 8-10.
n.a. Not available.
a. Trend values.
b. For human consumption.
c. Past growth rates for all foods are probably not significantly greater than those for foodgrains.
d. Increase in weather-adjusted yields, 1966–67 to 1977–78, was 2.8 percent for all cereals (see chapter 8).

growth will accelerate substantially in the next quarter century. It is also subject to an upward bias in our estimates of demand as a function of income: per capita food demand is not likely to rise to 3,400 calories, even at the projected income level.

Our analysis suggests, nevertheless, that even this high projected demand could be satisfied from domestic production, assuming (1) further growth of irrigation at a slightly higher rate than in the past; (2) accelerated growth of double cropping; and (3) a sixfold increase in fertilizer use, which actually would imply an annual growth rate lower than past or current rates.

There is only one other set of projections extending to the end of the century comparable to ours, that of the National Commission on Agriculture.[1] As can be seen from table 9-2, the NCA's conclusions are similar to ours, despite some differences in assumptions and methodology. The NCA projects a lower rate of population growth. Its projected rate of urbanization is intermediate between our high income-growth (alternative A) and low income-growth (C + D) assumptions (chapter 7); the same is true of the top of its income-growth range. Although the NCA's estimates of per capita foodgrain demand are somewhat higher than ours at comparable income levels, the total demand projected by the NCA is similar to ours. The NCA does not project the total demand for calories from all foods, but its projections of demand for specific foodstuffs, such as fats and oils and sugar, also indicate a more rapid increase in the consumption of such foods than that projected for foodgrains. As in this study, the NCA anticipates that the prospective demand for foodgrains can be met from domestic production. The NCA's projections for net cropped area, gross cropped area, and yields of foodgrains are virtually identical with our estimates. The NCA projects a somewhat greater increase in net irrigated area but a smaller increase in the degree of double cropping of irrigated land. The NCA expects fertilizer consumption to increase fivefold, instead of the sixfold increase projected here.

The Food and Agriculture Organization has projected food demand to 1985 and 2000 and food production to 1985.[2] Like NCA, FAO projects a somewhat lower rate of population growth than we do. Its income-growth projection corresponds roughly to our low income-growth variant.

1. *Report of the National Commission on Agriculture*, pt. 3: *Demand and Supply*, Government of India, Ministry of Agriculture and Irrigation (Delhi: Controller of Publications, 1976).

2. Unpublished data, Food and Agriculture Organization of the United Nations.

Table 9-2. *Authors' Projections Compared with Projections by the National Commission on Agriculture, India, 1975–2000*

Item	Projections for 2000[a]		Average annual growth rate, 1975–2000 (percent)[a]	
	Authors'	NCA	Authors'	NCA
Population (millions)	993	935	2.0	1.7
Urban population (percent of total)	41	29	2.5 (0.0)	1.1
Income per capita (1975 = 100)	239 (156)[b]	166 (110)[c]	3.5 (1.6)	2.1 (0.4)
Per capita foodgrain demand (kilograms per year)[d]	191 (181)	195 (180)	0.5 (0.3)	0.6 (0.3)
Total foodgrain demand (millions of metric tons per year)[e]	220 (202)	225 (205)	2.5 (2.3)	2.7 (2.3)
Foodgrain production (millions of metric tons per year)	220	230	2.4	2.6
Foodgrain yields (kilograms per hectare)	1,889	1,870	2.8	2.8
Gross cropped area (millions of hectares)	203	200	0.7	0.7
Net cropped area (millions of hectares)	144	150	0.0	0.2
Cropping intensity, total (percent)	141	133	0.6	0.5
Gross irrigated area (millions of hectares)	94	84	3.1	2.7
Net irrigated area (millions of hectares)	57	61	2.1	2.4
Irrigated cropping intensity (percent)	165	138	1.1	0.4
Fertilizer consumption (millions of metric tons per year)	17.8	14–16	7.1	6.4–6.9

Sources: Authors' projections, tables 7-2, 7-3, 7-4, 7-7, 8-4, 8-7, 8-10; *Report of the National Commission on Agriculture*, pt. 3: *Demand and Supply*, Government of India, Ministry of Agriculture and Irrigation (Delhi: Controller of Publications, 1976), tables 10.2, 10.6, 10.8, 10.9, 11.4, 11.6, 11.11, 11.13, pp. 10, 14, 16, 23, 61, 65, 76, and 80; growth rates, authors' calculations.

a. Low income-growth assumption in parentheses (authors' projections under alternative C + D).
b. Rural, 223 (149); urban, 223 (149).
c. Rural, 149 (116); urban, 172 (136).
d. For human consumption.
e. All uses.

At these lower income-growth rates, FAO projects a more rapid growth of per capita demand for foodgrains but slower growth rates for other foods. Because of the population factor, the projected growth of total foodgrain requirements is roughly the same (table 9-3).

The USDA and IFPRI studies[3] assume a higher rate of population growth (2.5 percent and 2.4 percent, respectively, following the UN medium projection) than we do. Both studies also expect higher rates of growth of demand for foodgrains than we do at comparable levels of income growth, but it is likely that this merely reflects the expectation that the pattern of food consumption will not change as much as projected here.

Most studies show the growth of foodgrain consumption corresponding closely to projected production, thus implying little change in import requirements. Only the IFPRI study shows demand running significantly ahead of production. The USDA's "accelerated growth of agricultural productivity," by contrast, shows production outpacing domestic demand.

In public discussions of projections of this kind, attention is generally focused on the magnitude of the "food gap" they predict. As can be seen from table 9-4, the estimates of India's net import requirements for foodgrains span a wide range, from a deficit of 22 million metric tons to a surplus of 3.6 million tons. However, not much significance should be attributed to such estimates, for two reasons. First, since the net deficit or surplus is small compared with production or consumption, even a slight error in estimating one or the other will have a disproportionately large impact on the residual. As a result, estimates of net import demand are subject to a wide margin of error. Second, in a large economy like India's, any significant, persistent imbalance between food production and consumption would set in motion economic and political forces that would tend to correct the imbalance. In the presence of foreign exchange constraints, prices would rise, which would stimulate production and restrain consumption; alternatively, the government might resort to rationing. Large food imports may materialize, however, if they are available at low cost and the balance-of-payments constraints are eased by export expansion or foreign aid, or both. For these reasons, no estimate of pro-

3. Anthony Rojko and others, *Alternative Futures for World Food in 1985,* vol. 1: *World GOL Model Analytical Report,* U.S. Department of Agriculture, Economics, Statistics, and Cooperative Service, Foreign Agricultural Report no. 146 (Government Printing Office, 1978); International Food Policy Research Institute, *Food Needs of Developing Countries: Projections of Production and Consumption to 1990,* Research Report 3 (Washington, D.C.: IFPRI, 1977).

Table 9-3. Projected Annual Growth Rates, India, Various Studies and Years

Item	Authors'[a]				FAO		USDA (1969–71 to 1985)[b]			IFPRI (1975–90)[a]	
	1975–90		1975–2000		1975–90	1975–2000	I	IV	IV-A	High	Low
	High	Low	High	Low						High	Low
Population	2.0	2.0	2.0	2.0	2.0	1.8	2.5	2.5	2.5	2.4	2.4
Income per capita	3.0	1.4	3.5	1.6	1.6	1.9	1.4	n.a.	n.a.	1.5	1.1
Per capita demand[c] for											
Foodgrains	0.7	0.2	0.5	0.3	0.4	0.5	0.5	1.3	1.5	0.7	0.5
Other vegetable foods	2.7	0.9	3.7	1.2	0.7	0.9	n.a.	n.a.	n.a.	n.a.	n.a.
Animal foods	4.7	3.1	5.0	2.4	0.9	1.2	n.a.	n.a.	n.a.	n.a.	n.a.
Total foodgrain demand	2.7	2.2	2.5	2.3	2.5	2.3	2.9	3.8	4.0	3.1	2.9
Foodgrain production	2.4	2.4	2.4	2.4	2.7[d]	n.a.	3.0	3.9	4.5	2.3	2.3

Source: Authors' projections, tables 7-2, 7-3, 7-4, 7-7, and 8-7. FAO projections, unpublished data, Food and Agriculture Organization of the United Nations. USDA projections, Anthony Rojko and others, *Alternative Futures for World Food in 1985*, vol. 1: *World GOL Model Analytical Report*, U.S. Department of Agriculture, Economics, Statistics, and Cooperative Service, Foreign Agricultural Report no. 146 (Government Printing Office, 1978), tables 3, 4, 16, 18, pp. 11, 13, 44, 46. IFPRI projections, International Food Policy Research Institute, *Food Needs of Developing Countries: Projections of Production and Consumption to 1990*, Research Report 3 (Washington, D.C.: IFPRI, 1977), table 10, p. 70; annex 4, tables 20–21, pp. 137, 147.

n.a. Not available.

a. High (low) income-growth assumptions are authors' alternative A, high income, and alternative C + D, low income (see chapter 7).

b. I represents a modified continuation of present trends in agricultural production and international trade policies; IV represents moderately higher productivity in the developing countries, high income growth, and high world demand; IV-A represents accelerated productivity in the developing countries, along with high income growth and world demand.

c. In terms of calories.

d. "Basic" (trend) assumption, 1972–74 to 1985.

Table 9-4. *Net Food Import Projections, India, Various Studies, 1985 or 1990*
Millions of metric tons

	Imports		
Study and year	Grains	Fats and oils	Sugar
FAO (1985)	3.4–5.5	2.6–2.8	−0.3–(−0.8)[a]
USDA[b]			
I (1985)	4.7	n.a.	n.a.
IV (1985)	6.0	n.a.	n.a.
IV-A (1985)	−3.6[a]	n.a.	n.a.
IFPRI			
Low income growth (1990)	17.6	n.a.	n.a.
High income growth (1990)	21.9	n.a.	n.a.

Sources: FAO projections, unpublished data; USDA projections, Rojko, *Alternative Futures for World Food in 1985*, vol. 1, table 15, p. 43; IFPRI projections, International Food Policy Research Institute, *Food Needs of Developing Countries*, table 10, p. 70.
a. Net exports.
b. Alternative scenarios defined in table 9-3.

spective imports is attempted here. We believe it is sufficient to show that, in this century at least, India can, with a slightly increased effort, produce enough food to satisfy any likely increase in demand.

The Role of Foreign Trade

While food self-sufficiency is clearly attainable in India, this does not mean that it should be the overriding goal of Indian policy to eliminate all food imports. India may well find its advantage in continuing to import some of its requirements for basic food staples that can be procured cheaply in the world market (such as grains and vegetable oils) while paying for these imports with the proceeds of its exports of labor-intensive agricultural and manufactured products. A look at India's present foreign trade pattern is instructive (table 9-5).

The future development of India's foreign trade will depend on the speed and direction of India's own economic growth, the competitiveness of its exports (which in turn will depend on its economic policies), and the willingness of other countries to keep their markets open to imports from developing countries. India's comparative advantage clearly lies in exporting labor-intensive agricultural and manufactured products. Increasingly, the traditional exports of textiles, clothing, and leather goods are being supplemented by more sophisticated industrial products. The

Table 9-5. *India's Exports and Imports, Annual Average, 1973–74 to 1975–76*
Billions of rupees

Item	Exports	Imports	Balance
Cereals and cereal products	0.2	8.6	−8.4
Meat, dairy, and fish	1.0	0.2	0.8
Fruits and vegetables	1.2	0.5	0.7
Sugar and sweeteners	2.9	0.0	2.9
Oilseeds and edible oils	0.8	0.2	0.6
All foods	6.1	9.5	−3.4
Tobacco and tobacco manufactures	0.8	0.0	0.8
Textile fibers	0.5	0.8	−0.3
Coffee, tea, cocoa	3.2	0.0	3.2
Jute	2.6	0.0	2.6
Agricultural nonfood	7.1	0.8	6.3
Total agricultural	13.2	10.3	2.9
Fertilizer	0.0	3.4	−3.4
Textile and leather, manufactures, handicrafts	7.1	0.0	7.1
Fuels	0.2	9.8	−9.6
Engineering products	3.2	7.9	−4.7
Total	33.0	42.5	−9.5

Source: Based on data in Government of India, *Economic Survey, 1977–78* (Delhi: Controller of Publications, 1978), pp. 41, 43.

main imports will continue to be fuels, raw materials, machinery, and equipment. India also imports about one-third of its fertilizer requirements at present but aims to become self-sufficient.

In the agricultural sector, India may be expected to continue to export tea. Jute exports, however, face increasing competition from synthetics. For most other agricultural products, India's net trade position will largely depend on domestic and foreign trade policies. India has been a net importer of foodgrains, cotton and, increasingly of late, of vegetable oils.[4] It is a net exporter of sugar, fruits and nuts, and tobacco. This pattern may change. India could become self-sufficient in grains, edible oils, and cotton. On the other hand, the growth of the domestic market could easily absorb the present surpluses of sugar, fruits and nuts, and tobacco.

But expanding export opportunities (for example, in the Middle East) could lead India in the opposite direction: expanded production of spe-

4. *Foreign Agriculture,* December 18, 1978, and May 1979.

cialized agricultural products for export and increased imports of grain and vegetable oils. Increased trade dependence would not necessarily mean that Indian agriculture, which is now virtually self-supporting (even if fertilizer imports are included), would become a burden on India's balance of payments; in fact, it is likely to make a modest positive contribution.

To sum up, India has some options in shaping its foreign trade policy: it may foster exports of manufactures, aim at a mix, import more food, or import less food. There is no reason for policymakers to think of the current pattern as the only possible or desirable one.

Investment Requirements

Foreign trade can help; but food imports can, at best, make only a marginal contribution to the total food supply of a country as large as India. In an average year, India imports less than 5 percent of its total food supply.

Meeting the projected increase in the demand for food will therefore require an accelerated agricultural development effort. This will not come cheaply or easily. While the major investment needs are for irrigation, fertilizer, and electrification, these programs must go hand-in-hand with improved crop protection, storage, and distribution. A major research effort is needed to maintain the momentum of genetic improvements; experience has shown that new varieties have to be introduced constantly if the gains already made are to be held and improved upon. Agricultural education and extension services are spread very thinly and require major expansion. Agricultural credit facilities must be made available to small farmers to enable them to take advantage of the new technology. Small farmers are also in need of cooperative arrangements for the purchase of inputs, the installation of tubewells, and the storage and marketing of farm produce.

The costs of the required investments are substantial. Capital requirements for new irrigation development may be estimated at roughly $45 billion (table 9-6). It is assumed, in this estimate, that the entire remaining tubewell potential, which requires less capital for development than large public water storage systems, will be exploited by the end of the century. There are several reasons other than lower costs per hectare for

Table 9-6. *Estimated Capital Costs[a] of Irrigation, India, 1975–2000*

Item	Major and medium irrigation	Minor irrigation	Total
New development			
Millions of gross hectares	27	24[b]	51
Cost per gross hectare (dollars)	1,300	400	875
Total cost (billions of dollars)	35.1	9.6	44.7
Improvement of existing systems			
Millions of gross hectares	17	26	43
Needing improvement	8.5	. . .	8.5
Cost per gross hectare (dollars)	300	. . .	300
Total cost (billions of dollars)	2.6	. . .	2.6
Replacement costs of tubewells[c]			
Needing replacement (millions of hectares)	. . .	62.5	62.5
Cost per gross hectare (dollars)	. . .	400	400
Total cost (billions of dollars)	. . .	25.0	25.0

Sources: Same as table 8-17.
a. In U.S. dollars of 1975 purchasing power.
b. Estimated remaining potential.
c. Tubewells assumed to require replacement after fifteen years. Area needing replacement will increase from 1.75 million hectares in 1975 to 3.35 million hectares in 2000, or an average of 2.5 million hectares per year.

stressing groundwater development.[5] Tubewells have the great advantage of providing water when needed. While public water supply systems can be designed in such a way as to make water supply more certain and available on demand, administrative reforms (such as metering) would be required that would be difficult to implement.

Further groundwater development will run up against new problems, however. As table 9-7 shows, the states that made rapid progress in groundwater development in the past—Punjab, Haryana, Gujarat, Rajasthan, and Tamil Nadu—have little or no scope for further growth. In the future, 90 percent of the groundwater development (14.8 million out of 16.4 million hectares remaining unexploited) will have to take place in those states, mainly in the Indo-Gangetic plain, where growth has been held back by a number of factors. First, most of the states in question have at least enough rainfall (75 centimeters or more) to produce one crop in the monsoon season (see table 9-7, column 5). The need for irrigation is, therefore, less compelling, even though it would provide insurance against a failure of the monsoon and, more important, open up the possibility of a second crop such as wheat or oilseeds in the dry season.

5. Though the capital cost advantage of tubewells will probably be more than offset by the energy costs of operating the pumps. See table 8-17.

Table 9-7. *Remaining Groundwater Potential and Factors Affecting Exploitation, by State, India*

State	Groundwater potential				Factors affecting exploitation		
	Total (1)	Exploited as of 1976–77 (2)	Area remaining (3)	Percent remaining (4)	Percent of gross cropped area with rainfall over 75 centimeters (5)	Percent of villages electrified (1977) (6)	Average size of holdings (hectares)[a] (7)
More potential							
Assam	0.6	0.0	0.6	100	100	9	1.5
Orissa	1.3	0.1	1.2	92	100	28	1.9
West Bengal	2.2	0.3	1.9	86	100	29	1.2
Bihar	3.6	1.0	2.6	72	100	27	1.5
Karnataka	1.4	0.4	1.0	71	35	55	3.2
Madhya Pradesh	2.6	0.9	1.7	65	96	20	4.0
Andhra Pradesh	1.9	0.8	1.1	58	66	50	2.5
Uttar Pradesh	11.4	6.7	4.7	41	84	29	1.2
Less potential							
Maharashtra	1.6	1.0	0.6	38	63	57	4.3
Tamil Nadu	1.3	1.1	0.2	15	100	99	1.5
Rajasthan	1.7	1.5	0.2	12	12	25	5.5
Gujarat	1.3	1.2	0.1	8	33	39	4.1
Punjab and Haryana	3.6	3.6	0.0	3	12	100	3.2
All India	35.0	18.6	16.4	47	67	35	2.3

Sources: Columns 1–4, unpublished data, Government of India, Ministry of Agriculture and Irrigation; columns 5 and 7, Government of India, Ministry of Agriculture and Irrigation, Directorate of Economics and Statistics, *Indian Agriculture in Brief*, 16th ed. (Delhi: Controller of Publications, 1978), table 2.6, pp. 32–33, and p. 75; column 6, unpublished data, Government of India, Ministry of Energy, Central Electricity Authority.

a. Census of 1970.

Second, rural electrification, essential to provide power for the pumpsets, is generally less advanced than in the states in which groundwater development was favored in the past. Third, the average size of holdings is generally smaller, so that there is a greater need for sharing of tubewell water among several farms. Though this can be done through cooperative or contract arrangements, these are not always easy to work out.

Our estimate for major and medium-size irrigation projects does not allow for the promising possibility, suggested by the Harvard Center for Population Studies, of storing water from the high flow of the Ganges (July through October) in the aquifer for use in the dry season.[6] This would be accomplished by pumping down the water table to a depth of about 30 meters so that more water could enter from the riverbed. The well field would be a storage corridor 6 kilometers wide on either side of the river; it would serve an irrigated area about 30 kilometers wide on either side. The system would provide an additional water supply on the order of 6 million hectare-meters. The project would involve the installation of 170,000 tubewells at an estimated cost of $1.7 billion and additional costs for distribution channels. The principal advantages of this approach are that it avoids the flooding of valuable river bottomland, siltage, and salination; it makes water available on demand; it lends itself to private use; and it can be divided into subprojects of limited size. Among the disadvantages is that underground storage does not provide power but uses it. Also, with the lowering of the water table, existing wells will have to be deepened.

An even more ambitious (and costly) scheme is now under study by the Government of India, the World Bank, and FAO.[7] It would link the water-short areas of central and southern India with the Brahmaputra and Ganges basins through a "garland" of canals connecting virtually all river systems.

In addition to the estimated $45 billion for new irrigation development, another $2 billion to $3 billion will be required for necessary improvements of the existing major and medium irrigation systems to reduce channel and field losses, to control salinity, and to increase the dependability of the water supply throughout the system and throughout the season. This will involve lining or compacting canals, repairing ditches and

6. Roger Revelle and V. Lakshminarayana, "The Ganges Water Machine," *Science*, vol. 188 (May 9, 1975), pp. 611–16. The annual mean low flow (November through June) provides no possibilities for additional irrigation since the present flow is needed for navigation and for irrigation in Bangladesh.

7. See *Hindu* (Madras), March 30, 1979, and *Times of India* (New Delhi), April 4, 1979.

turnouts, leveling or terracing fields, and installing tubewells to supplement canal water supplies (see chapter 8). With such improvements, the efficiency of the present surface irrigation system could ultimately be increased from about 30 percent to 50 percent, groundwater use efficiency from about 50 percent to 70 percent, and average irrigation efficiency from 40 percent to 60 percent. But perhaps all that can realistically be hoped for by the year 2000 is a surface water efficiency of 35 percent, a groundwater efficiency of 60 percent, and a weighted average efficiency of about 50 percent.[8]

Because of the relatively short life of tubewells (assumed to be fifteen years), we have made an additional allowance for the cost of replacing them, amounting to $25 billion. Total capital costs of irrigation, including this item, are therefore on the order of $75 billion (table 9-6).

In 1975, India used 3 million tons of fertilizer (in terms of pure nutrients), of which about 1 million tons were imported. Its total production capacity (about 2.5 million tons) was not fully utilized. By the end of the century, fertilizer use is projected to reach 17.8 million tons (see table 9-2). Assuming that all of this is produced domestically, and capacity utilization rises to 90 percent, an additional capacity for 17.2 million tons is required. The total investment cost, at about $800 per ton of capacity, would be $13.8 billion.

Other investment requirements are more difficult to gauge. Perhaps as much as $1 billion annually, or $25 billion over the twenty-five-year period, may be required for rural electrification, roads, storage facilities, and other infrastructure investments. Total agricultural investment requirements would thus amount to about $115 billion, or $4.5 billion annually, in 1975 dollars.[9]

Increased Government Support for Agricultural Investment

The need for increased emphasis on food production has been recognized in India's new development plan.[10] Agriculture's share is scheduled

8. Based on Conference on the Economics of Irrigation, Tucson, Arizona, March 1–2, 1976, summary, table 3. Averages based on relative weights of major and minor irrigation in India in 1975.

9. This may be compared with a $3.4 billion annual rate of agricultural outlays in the Fifth Plan and a $5 billion annual rate (1978 dollars) in the Sixth Plan (see table 2-1). Rupee values converted to dollars at 8:1 for 1974–77 and 8.5:1 for 1978–83.

10. Government of India, Planning Commission, *Draft Five Year Plan, 1978–83* (Delhi: Controller of Publications, 1978).

to increase from 27.7 percent of the total plan outlay to 30.8 percent (see table 2-1). In addition, the share devoted to social expenditures in rural areas[11] will increase, from about 10 percent to 12 percent.

The new plan foresees an increase in the gross irrigated area from 48 million hectares in 1977–78 to 63 million hectares in 1982–83; this represents an annual rate of growth of 5.5 percent, which would be the highest achieved in any quinquennium. About half of the additional irrigated area would be from major and medium projects and half from minor irrigation, a distribution consistent with our projections. Of the 8 million hectares in major and medium projects, 6 million are to come from ongoing projects, 1.4 million from new projects, and 0.6 million from the modernization of existing systems. About 80 percent of the additional minor irrigation is to come from groundwater development, the remainder from minor surface irrigation works.

The funds allocated for major and medium irrigation in the new plan amount to 79.25 billion rupees ($9.0 billion)—well over twice the 34.3 billion rupees provided in the Fifth Plan. A large part of this increase reflects increased costs. During the Fifth Plan period the average cost, mostly for ongoing projects, was 5,700 rupees per hectare. The Sixth Plan implies an average cost of about 10,000 rupees per hectare ($1,176), which is still low compared with construction costs elsewhere. The area earmarked for modernization (600,000 hectares) seems surprisingly small, considering that this is undoubtedly the most cost-effective way of increasing the total supply and, at the same time, improving the seasonal and geographic distribution of irrigation water. Minor irrigation projects are financed only partly by the public sector. The new plan provides for public sector outlays of 17.3 billion rupees, more than twice the 7.9 billion rupees provided in the Fifth Plan.

The plan proposes to raise the consumption of chemical fertilizers from 4.2 million tons (NPK) in 1977–78 to 7.8 million tons in 1982–83 —an annual growth rate of 13.3 percent, as compared with 10 percent achieved during the Fifth Plan.

The new plan calls for the electrification of 100,000 villages and 2,000,000 pumpsets, as compared with 80,000 villages and 900,000 pumpsets in 1974–78. The plan provides 14.5 billion rupees for this pur-

---

11. Electric power and water for rural households, roads, health and family welfare, education, nutrition, housing, social welfare, and traditional cottage and household industries.

pose, with an additional 3 billion rupees to come from commercial banks and other financial institutions. The proportion of villages electrified, which rose from 8 to 35 percent between 1966 and 1977, is projected to reach 56 percent by 1983.

The new plan proposes to double the credit available to farmers in the next three years from the current level of 23 billion rupees, with increased emphasis on credit cooperatives.

The allocation of funds for research has also been doubled, from 2.1 billion rupees in the Fifth Plan to $4.25 billion in the new plan. A National Agricultural Research Fund has been established, with support from the World Bank, to assist the agricultural universities in carrying out location-specific research.

The "training and visits" systems of agricultural extension (see chapter 5) will be expanded to cover 22 million farms (31 percent of all farms) as compared with 9 million farms at present.

As a result of this effort, the government expects a 6.1 million hectare increase in the multiple cropped area, a 15 million hectare increase in the area planted to high-yielding varieties of grain, and a total production of 140 million tons of foodgrains by 1982–83. Both the input targets and the anticipated 3.3 to 3.9 percent annual increase in foodgrain production seem optimistic.[12]

The target for oilseeds calls for a 4 percent annual growth rate—more than three times that recorded in the past five years. Increased emphasis on oil-bearing crops is a response to the growing gap between demand and production, which led to sharply increased imports of vegetable oils in 1976–77 and 1977–78.[13] Imports are likely to continue to rise even if the new plan's goal is achieved. Sugar production is projected to expand by 3.7 percent a year, about the same rate as in the past five years.[14]

On the whole, the government, though probably too ambitious, seems to have its priorities right. There is every reason to expect that increased

12. Calculated from trend production (119.5 million metric tons) rather than actual production (125 million metric tons) in base year 1978–79 (see table 2-2). The plan document's longer term projection, of 164 million to 169 million metric tons in 1987–88, is in line with our projection of 173 million metric tons for 1990 (see table 8-10).

13. Imports of edible vegetable oils climbed from 105,000 metric tons in 1975–76 to 770,000 tons in 1976–77 and 1,280,000 tons in 1977–78. See *Foreign Agriculture,* December 18, 1978, and May 1979.

14. "Indian Plan Targets Sharp Crop Gains," ibid., December 18, 1978, pp. 8–10.

attention to agriculture will result in accelerated growth of food production in the next five years.

Price Policy and Supply Management

India's food policy will continue to operate under the same economic and political constraints as in the past. It must provide adequate incentives to producers and, at the same time, ensure a minimum level of nutrition to the poor at prices they can afford. Food imports will continue to be limited by balance-of-payments constraints; subsidies to producers and consumers will be limited by budgetary constraints. Given these constraints, it is not surprising that Indian food policy has not changed a great deal since independence.

It is often said that Indian objectives would be served better by higher price supports, increased input subsidies, reduced food imports, or some combination of these. Advocates of this strategy believe that it would stimulate domestic food production and increase food supplies. This outcome is not self-evident, however. The available evidence suggests that farmers' returns have been more than sufficient to cover the costs of increased quantities of fertilizer and other inputs as they became available. Irrigation and fertilizer availabilities and the farmer's access to technology and credit seem rather to have been the limiting factors.

Higher prices would not remove these impediments. But higher food prices *would* affect food consumption patterns: the result would be higher consumption in the countryside and lower consumption in the cities. The poor, who even now cannot afford a minimum diet, would be most seriously affected. High agricultural support prices are a luxury which poor countries cannot afford.

This also applies to subsidies. The Indian farmer is already being assisted by government-subsidized water and fertilizer. Land taxes are very low. But budgetary constraints will continue to limit government outlays for subsidies.

Clearly, India does not have the policy options available to affluent countries such as Japan or Western European countries. It must husband its resources carefully. Barring emergencies, it is better to reserve scarce public funds for economic development.

While India's food policy is sound in principle, there is room for improvement in the way it is managed. Food supplies and prices could have been more stable if there had been better timing of imports and government stock movements.[15] Whether primary reliance should be placed on imports or stock management is a widely debated question[16] which is not easy to answer at this time because of uncertainties concerning future international arrangements to improve "food security." A national grain reserve adequate to meet worst-case contingencies such as the two successive crop failures of 1965–66 and 1966–67 is costly to maintain.[17] An optimal national stock would probably be less than half this size, with the remaining shortfalls being made up by imports.[18] Reliance on imports may seem unwise, however, so long as there is a serious risk of recurring worldwide shortages. India's experience in 1973–76, when it was faced

15. John Wall ("Foodgrain Management: Pricing, Procurement, Distribution, Import and Storage Policy," in *India: Occasional Papers,* World Bank Staff Working Paper 279 [World Bank, 1978], pp. 43–91) shows, for example, that average per capita foodgrain supplies could have been maintained at 425 grams per day (rising from 400 grams in 1951 to 450 grams in 1976) with less than half the actual level of imports. This would have required heavier stockpiling in years of above-average production, with government stocks reaching a peak of 18 million tons in 1964–65. Imports would have been necessary in only seven years, with peaks of 11.6 million tons in 1966–67 and 9.3 million tons in 1974–75 (table 1, p. 91).

16. See, for example, Shlomo Reutlinger and others, "Should Developing Nations Carry Grain Reserves?" in David J. Eaton and W. Scott Steele, comps., *Analyses of Grain Reserves, A Proceedings,* U.S. Department of Agriculture, Economic Research Service, in cooperation with the National Science Foundation, ERS report 634 (USDA, 1976), pp. 12–38; D. Gale Johnson and David Sumner, "An Optimization Approach to Grain Reserves for Developing Countries," in ibid., pp. 56–76; Food and Agriculture Organization of the United Nations, "Report of the Expert Consultation on Cereal Stock Policies Relating to World Food Security," ESC:WFS 75/4 (April 1975), presented to the Ad Hoc Consultation on World Food Security, Rome, May 19–23, 1975; Panos Konandreas, Barbara Huddleston, and Virabongsa Ramangkura, *Food Security: An Insurance Approach,* International Food Policy Research Institute, Research Report 4 (Washington, D.C.: IFPRI, 1978).

17. Foodgrain production in these two years combined was 25 million tons below trend. For a reserve with this capacity, storage costs alone would be roughly $200 million per year. Assuming an average inventory of 15 million tons, interest costs (at 10 percent a year) would add another $150 million. This would be partly offset by the annualized gains on resale (which could be substantial if the stocks were acquired on concessional terms).

18. In the example given by Wall, average stocks would have been only 5 million tons ("Foodgrain Management," p. 91). Reutlinger concludes that "a 10 million buffer stock, operated in a manner to take advantage of opportunity to import when world prices are low for a later year, [would] practically [pay] for itself" (p. 97). Remaining import needs could be financed from a modest foreign-exchange reserve set aside for this purpose. See Shlomo Reutlinger, "The Level and Stability of India's Foodgrain Consumption," in *India: Occasional Papers,* World Bank Staff Working Paper 279 (World Bank, 1978), pp. 92–123.

with the necessity of importing large quantities of grain at the then-prevailing high world prices, was undoubtedly a contributing factor in the government's decision to carry larger stocks.[19]

The case for relying on imports rather than national grain reserves to meet emergencies would be much stronger if India could be assured of access to world grain supplies at reasonable prices, as well as to international credit to help pay for emergency imports whenever the need arose. An international system of wheat reserves, for which negotiations are to be resumed, would help to stabilize world supplies and prices. The emergency wheat reserve proposed by the Carter administration would help maintain food aid shipments in periods of worldwide shortage or increase them to meet crop shortfalls in developing countries. International Monetary Fund credit facilities could help to finance emergency food imports. If adequate international arrangements can be worked out, it may well be to India's advantage to reduce its national grain reserve to not more than 10 million tons capacity.

Ensuring a Minimum Level of Nutrition

Even on the most favorable assumptions regarding income growth and food supply, some 5 percent of India's population—50 million people—may still be undernourished at the end of the century (see chapter 7). There will thus be a continuing need for special programs to ensure a minimum level of nutrition for those who are unable to meet their essential food needs.

The Indian food distribution system has demonstrated its capacity to deal with emergencies. There has been no massive starvation since the Bengal famine of 1943, which cost the lives of an estimated 1.5 million people.[20] Improved transportation and international trade and food aid, together with government efforts to ensure a minimum food supply to the areas and people in greatest need, helped avoid disaster in the droughts of 1965–66 and 1966–67, which affected several states;[21] in Maharashtra in

19. It is likely, however, that the government did not intend stocks to be as large as were actually accumulated (see chapter 4).

20. Unofficial estimates put the death toll, including deaths from famine-induced diseases, at 2.5 million to 4 million.

21. See Alan Berg, "Famine Contained: Notes and Lessons from the Bihar Experience," in *Famine: A Symposium Dealing with Nutrition and Relief Operations in Times of Disaster,* edited by Gunnar Blix, Yngve Hofvander, and Bo Vahlquist

1972–73; in West Bengal during the influx of millions of refugees from Bangladesh in 1971; and again following the harvest failure of 1974. In all these cases, millions of people suffered severe privation, but the relief efforts succeeded in averting the worst.

The system has also helped to mitigate the widespread undernutrition that is endemic in the countryside as well as in the cities. The major limitation of the existing food programs—fair-price shops and special programs for the aged and infirm, children, and expectant and nursing mothers—is that they are largely confined to the urban centers. Both rural and urban areas are served by supplementary employment programs, such as the employment guarantee program in the state of Maharashtra,[22] which indirectly help to maintain a minimum level of food consumption; but the scope and effectiveness of these programs vary a great deal from state to state, and they fall far short of reaching all needy people.

Greatly increased public expenditure programs serving basic human needs can be justified not only from a political and humanitarian point of view, but also in terms of their impact on economic development. Human capital is a country's most important resource. In India, improved nutrition would pay enormous dividends in terms of increased human productivity. "Improved nutrition that returns an absent worker to the active labor force, or helps lengthen his working life span, or overcomes a debility that is reducing his productive capacity, or that enables a child to return to school or to improve his understanding or retention of things taught, or that enables an adult to absorb more effectively in-service training or the advice of an agricultural extension agent clearly raises the flow of earnings above what it would have been in absence of the improvement in well-being."[23]

While there is a definite need for special programs to assure a minimum

---

for the Swedish Nutrition Foundation and the Swedish International Development Authority (Uppsala, Sweden: SNF, 1971), pp. 113–29 (Brookings Reprint 211). While paying tribute to government efforts, Berg also draws attention to the important role of voluntary agencies (CARE and several religious groups), which proved to be extremely effective in cutting red tape and setting standards of efficiency in food distribution.

22. See Inderjit Singh, "Small Farms and the Landless in South Asia," World Bank Staff Working Paper 320 (February 1979), annex 3.

23. Alan Berg, *The Nutrition Factor: Its Role in National Development* (Brookings Institution, 1973), p. 17. Next to food, one of the most urgent problems, particularly in rural areas, is a dependable supply of safe drinking water. The relatively modest public expenditures required for this purpose would yield large returns in terms of improved public health.

level of nutrition, there may be ways of improving their effectiveness. A strong case can be made for much greater reliance on public works programs that serve both developmental and nutritional needs. The additional demand for food generated by these programs could be met from existing stocks, increased domestic production, and international food aid.

With more ample food supplies, the government procurement system has—temporarily, at least—turned into a price support system. The effective demand for food, at present prices, is insufficient to absorb the surplus. This situation is likely to change, however, as a result of crop shortfalls or because of increased demand generated by more rapid income growth. If food supplies become tight again, it will be desirable to avoid, so far as possible, renewed resort to coercive government procurement and internal barriers to foodgrain trade. To this end, the Indian government should not hesitate to draw on its excess stocks and to take advantage of international food aid.

The Role of International Assistance

International assistance will continue to be required to support the agricultural development effort. From 1973 to 1976, the average annual capital commitment in aid to agriculture and fertilizer production in India was as follows:[24]

Source of assistance	Millions of U.S. dollars
DAC countries	81.3
International institutions	307.1
Total	388.4

The total of under $400 million annually represents only a small fraction of total annual investment requirements of about $4 billion to $5 billion.[25] About three-fourths of this assistance was channeled through the World Bank and the International Development Association. World Bank–IDA

24. Includes assistance for forestry, fisheries, fertilizer supply and production, food processing, and rural development. Excludes food aid other than that of the World Food Program. See Consultative Group on Food Production and Investment in Developing Countries, "Analysis of Resource Flows in Agriculture, 1973–76," Washington, D.C., March 1978, annex 2, table 6, p. 6.

DAC countries are member countries of the Development Assistance Committee of the Organisation for Economic Co-operation and Development.

25. On a per capita basis, foreign aid to Indian agriculture was only about half of the average level of foreign agricultural assistance to eighteen priority food-deficit developing countries. See "Analysis of Resource Flows in Agriculture, 1973–76," annex 2, table 6, p. 6.

agricultural commitments rose more than fivefold between fiscal years 1973 and 1979 (table 9-8), but the increase is only about half that if allowance is made for the 100 percent rise in the international price level.[26] Clearly, a much higher level of international assistance would be desirable.

Table 9-8. *World Bank Loans and International Development Association Credits for Indian Agriculture, Commitments, Fiscal Years 1973–79*
Millions of U.S. dollars

	Type of assistance				
Fiscal year	Agriculture and rural development	Fertilizer	Total agriculture and fertilizer	Total loans and credits	Agriculture and fertilizer as percent of total
1973	79	58	137	564	24
1974	127	50	177	442	40
1975	340	200	540	840	64
1976	192	105	297	894	33
1977	321	...	321	750	43
1978	664	...	664	1,282	52
1979	520	250	770	1,492	52
Total	2,243	663	2,906	6,264	47

Source: World Bank, *Annual Report, 1978*, and preceding issues for years shown.

In addition, India is receiving food aid, but on a much smaller scale than in the mid-sixties, when the United States alone supplied about 500 million dollars' worth annually. In 1974–78, the annual flow of food aid from all sources probably did not exceed $200 million, including about $100 million donated by the United States under title II of Public Law 480 (the Food for Peace program) and $30 million supplied under title I. These programs are exceedingly modest when compared with the food needs of the 200 million undernourished people in India. In view of the food surpluses again being accumulated in the United States and elsewhere and the costly efforts to restrict production, it would seem to make sense to step up substantially the flow of food aid to India.

26. See Organisation for Economic Co-operation and Development, *Development Co-operation: Efforts and Policies of the Members of the Development Assistance Committee, 1978 Review* (Paris: OECD, 1978), table A-8, pp. 196–97. Deflator converted to fiscal years and extended to fiscal 1979 on basis of index of unit prices of exports of industrial countries (from International Monetary Fund, *International Financial Statistics*).

It is often argued that providing aid in the form of food is undesirable because of its alleged adverse effects on the demand for, and supply of, domestic food. It can be shown, however, that such disincentive effects can be avoided[27] if, first, food aid is channeled primarily to the poor, at low cost; in effect, this increases the incomes of the poor, since the major proportion of their additional income is spent on food. Second, proceeds of the sale of food supplied by food aid are used to finance job-creating investments; this generates additional income. In India, about 40 to 50 percent of the additional income is spent on food. Third, sales proceeds are used to increase agricultural productivity.

In the first two cases, food aid creates additional demand for food. In the third case, it also reduces the farmer's unit cost and hence his break-even price. Given the high income elasticity of demand at low income levels, it is likely that up to 40 percent of development aid could be provided in the form of food without affecting the aggregate demand for, or supply of, domestic food. A lower percentage of food aid in the total aid package would be desirable, however, to leave room for additional expansion of domestic food production. Food aid can support such expansion directly if the sales proceeds are earmarked for investments in agriculture.

Some policy changes are necessary if food aid is to become an effective tool of economic development. India, like many other developing countries, has been reluctant to rely on food aid so long as the flow of food aid is subject to economic and political uncertainties. Recipient countries will hesitate to increase food rations and set aside sales proceeds for public works and other development projects unless supplies are assured for a definite number of years.[28] Care should be taken to ensure, at the same time, that the availability of food aid does not lead the government of the recipient country to neglect the agricultural sector. Incentives can be provided to encourage the use of sales proceeds for agricultural development;[29] but the ultimate test is the makeup of the overall investment plan.

There is no convincing evidence that food aid has discouraged agricul-

27. See, for example, Uma K. Srivastava and others, *Food Aid and International Economic Growth* (Iowa State University Press, 1975).

28. This has been recommended in a task force report to the U.S. Secretary of Agriculture, *New Directions for U.S. Food Assistance: A Report of the Special Task Force on the Operation of Public Law 480* (USDA, 1978), pp. 34, 54–75.

29. Since 1966, U.S. food aid has been conditional upon "self-help" measures by the recipient country to increase food production. The 1977 legislation (International Development and Food Assistance Act of 1977, P.L. 95-88) permits the transfer of food aid on a grant basis if the sales proceeds are earmarked for agricultural and rural development.

tural production in India or that it has caused the Indian government to deemphasize agricultural development. On the contrary, the country's heavy dependence on food aid in the mid-sixties, accompanied as it was by an abundance of foreign advice and admonitions, seems to have stimulated the drive for self-sufficiency. This has had favorable effects in leading to greater emphasis on food production. It has also contributed to the government's decision to build up very large reserves rather than releasing the excess supplies for consumption. An assured flow of food aid and provisions for an automatic increase in food aid in years of crop shortfalls would undoubtedly make it easier for the government of India to liberalize the food distribution system and expand its supplementary employment programs.

We have dwelt on food aid at some length because it has been controversial. We believe that, with proper precautions, food aid can be an effective supplement to other forms of foreign economic assistance. To avoid disincentive effects on domestic agricultural development, it should probably not exceed one-third of total aid.

We have not discussed another controversial issue—whether foreign aid should be used as a lever to reduce economic and social inequalities in the recipient country; to promote employment, if necessary, at the cost of efficiency; and to encourage land reform. Indian politicians on both sides of the aisle are aware of the social problems of their highly stratified and still semifeudal society. The record of successive Indian governments, while far from perfect, compares well with that of many other countries at comparable stages of economic development. Remoteness from the scene, as well as the limited leverage provided by rather marginal foreign assistance, would seem to suggest that foreign governments would be wise to exercise self-restraint in offering advice in this difficult area of national policy.

In any event, debates over fine points in the direction of the development effort should not obscure the need for a substantial increase in the volume of aid. In 1977, the total net flow of foreign assistance to India was just over $1 billion—only $1.60 for every Indian, or 1 percent of India's gross national product. It represents a much smaller share in the total aid flow (5.5 percent) than would be indicated by India's share (about 50 percent) in the population of low-income aid-receiving countries.

Paradoxically, India is paying a penalty for its responsible—some would say, excessively conservative—fiscal and development policies and their success in restraining inflation and imports and stimulating exports.

In the past few years, India's foreign exchange reserves soared from $1.4 billion in 1975 to almost $7 billion in 1978, despite increased costs of oil imports. Inevitably, given the country's strong balance-of-payments and reserve position, it is difficult to make a case for increased foreign assistance. In fact, India's net aid receipts have declined sharply since 1976, when they amounted to $1.8 billion, or 10 percent of the total net flow of international assistance.[30]

Foreign observers naturally hesitate to criticize a policy of self-reliance that has long been held up as a model to developing countries. India's policymakers, for their part, have been reluctant to rely on increased international assistance, which they fear might bring foreign interference in the country's internal affairs. They have been even more reluctant to give a role to private foreign capital.

But what we have said of food aid also applies to aid in general. There can be little doubt that greatly increased foreign resources could be used to good effect. India, more than most developing countries, has the administrative capacity to channel additional resources into productive uses. On the basis of past performance, there is little ground for concern that increased aid would deflect the government from its essentially sound development policies.

An increased flow of foreign resources, including selective private investments, would enable India to maintain significantly higher rates of economic growth than would otherwise be possible. The fear that this would entail political dependence is a carryover from the past that has lost most of its validity. Foreign assistance—increasingly supplied under the auspices of the World Bank, the regional banks, and other international organizations, or of international consortia of bilateral donors— has been largely depoliticized. Private foreign investors, no longer able to count on unconditional support from their home governments, have become more flexible and accommodating in dealing with host countries. Last but not least, India now is a world power quite able to protect its own interests.

30. Organisation for Economic Co-operation and Development, *Development Co-operation*, table D. 3, p. 235.

Statistical Data

Table A-1. *Rainfall Indexes, Various Crops, India, 1951–52 to 1977–78*

Year	All cereals	Wheat[a]	Rice[b]
		Crop	
1951–52	82	...	...
1952–53	95	...	...
1953–54	103	...	...
1954–55	96	...	...
1955–56	109	...	...
1956–57	119	...	...
1957–58	85	82.80	84.60
1958–59	101	97.74	88.98
1959–60	106	113.40	103.32
1960–61	102	122.62	105.27
1961–62	100	129.95	106.81
1962–63	94	98.99	93.51
1963–64	96	103.54	105.51
1964–65	105	115.50	102.67
1965–66	74	66.14	82.49
1966–67	83	82.41	87.20
1967–68	103	117.65	98.14
1968–69	89	84.95	96.35
1969–70	99	99.66	103.32
1970–71	104	101.67	104.13
1971–72	104	113.98	114.67
1972–73	84	77.92	93.19
1973–74	103	104.81	117.26
1974–75	87	77.25	93.19
1975–76	110	110.52	110.78
1976–77	90	102.61	92.30
1977–78	100	95.86	116.29

Sources: Ralph W. Cummings, Jr., and S. K. Ray, "1968–69 Foodgrain Production: Relative Contribution of Weather and New Technology," *Economic and Political Weekly*, Review of Agriculture, September 27, 1969, pp. A-163–A-174, extended through 1977–78; rainfall data, *Agricultural Situation in India,* issues for years shown (New Delhi: Government of India, Ministry of Agriculture and Irrigation, Directorate of Economics and Statistics), rainfall estimates.

a. Rainfall indexes for wheat calculated as follows: (1) rainfall data, reported for thirty-one major zones, were combined into state averages by weighting each zone by its cultivated area; (2) the total quantity of rainfall affecting wheat production (June–February) was calculated for each major wheat growing state; (3) state rainfall figures were combined into all-India averages by weighting each year's rainfall in the wheat growing states by their wheat production in that year; (4) the all-India averages were converted into percentages of the normal (= 100), based on the average of twenty years (1957–58 to 1976–77). Rainfall indexes were not prepared for the period before 1957–58, as the areas covered under some rainfall reporting zones were different and hence not comparable with those for later years.

b. Calculated as for wheat (see note a). Rainfall relevant to the rice crop is March–December.

Table A-2. *Yields and Factors Affecting Yields, All Cereals, India,
1951–52 to 1977–78*

Year	Yield (kilograms per hectare)	Rainfall index	Gross irrigated area (millions of hectares)[a]	Fertilizer use[b] on cereals (kilograms per hectare)
1951–52	588	82	18.20	...
1952–53	633	95	19.00	0.59
1953–54	714	103	20.00	0.84
1954–55	687	96	20.10	0.98
1955–56	669	109	20.60	1.05
1956–57	687	119	20.40	1.22
1957–58	644	85	21.20	1.48
1958–59	723	101	21.50	1.73
1959–60	710	106	21.84	2.34
1960–61	758	102	22.06	2.23
1961–62	762	100	22.45	2.89
1962–63	716	94	23.39	3.57
1963–64	753	96	23.34	4.31
1964–65	810	105	23.94	4.84
1965–66	667	74	24.02	5.73
1966–67	696	83	25.79	8.27
1967–68	849	103	26.10	10.90
1968–69	820	89	28.05	11.81
1969–70	872	99	29.55	13.70
1970–71	920	104	30.12	15.00
1971–72	908	104	30.54	18.22
1972–73	853	84	30.74	19.50
1973–74	902	103	31.17	18.89
1974–75	874	87	33.26	18.38
1975–76	1,040	110	34.08	19.56
1976–77	984	90	n.a.	23.55
1977–78	1,098[c]	100	n.a.	29.11[c]

Sources: Government of India, Ministry of Agriculture and Irrigation, Directorate of Economics and Statistics, *Estimates of Area and Production of Principal Crops in India, 1977–78* (Delhi: Controller of Publications, 1979); and Fertilizer Association of India, *Fertilizer Statistics,* issues for years shown. Yields calculated on the basis of index numbers of yields. Rainfall index, from table A-1.

n.a. Not available.

a. For all foodgrains.

b. Assumes that 70 percent of total fertilizer use is devoted to cereals.

c. Preliminary.

Table A-3. *Gross Cropped Area, Net Cropped Area, and Cropping Intensity, India, 1950–51 to 1975–76*

Year	Gross cropped area (millions of hectares)	Net cropped area (millions of hectares)	Cropping intensity index[a]
1950–51	131.89	118.75	111
1951–52	133.23	119.40	112
1952–53	137.67	123.44	112
1953–54	142.48	126.81	112
1954–55	144.09	127.84	113
1955–56	147.31	129.16	114
1956–57	149.49	130.85	114
1957–58	145.83	129.08	113
1958–59	151.63	131.83	115
1959–60	152.82	132.94	115
1960–61	152.77	133.20	115
1961–62	156.21	135.40	115
1962–63	156.76	136.34	115
1963–64	156.96	136.48	115
1964–65	159.23	138.12	115
1965–66	155.28	136.20	114
1966–67	157.35	137.23	115
1967–68	163.74	139.88	117
1968–69	159.53	137.31	116
1969–70	162.26	138.77	117
1970–71	165.79	140.78	118
1971–72	165.15	140.22	118
1972–73	162.14	137.59	118
1973–74	169.56	142.76	119
1974–75	163.86	138.12	119
1975–76	170.99	142.22	120

Source: *Estimates of Area and Production, 1977–78*, app. 1, p. 145. Figures for 1976–77 and 1977–78 are not available.

a. Ratio of gross cropped area to net cropped area, times 100.

Table A-4. *Expenditure per Capita on Roots, Vegetables, Fruits, Nuts, Sugar, and Edible Oils, by Expenditure Class, India, 1964–65*
Amounts in rupees per year

Expenditure class	Total population		Rural population		Urban population	
	Percent in class	Expen-diture	Percent in class	Expen-diture	Percent in class	Expen-diture
0–96	1.3	8.24	1.5	8.03	0.5	10.71
96–132	4.6	13.20	5.1	12.90	2.3	16.18
132–156	5.2	15.13	5.8	14.60	3.0	19.47
156–180	6.8	18.58	7.3	17.76	4.9	23.72
180–216	11.6	22.09	12.1	21.17	9.4	27.13
216–252	12.3	26.30	12.8	25.06	10.0	33.09
252–288	11.2	32.22	11.6	31.02	9.7	38.32
288–336	11.8	36.43	11.8	34.55	11.5	44.53
336–408	12.7	43.55	12.5	40.88	13.6	54.02
408–516	10.0	53.19	9.6	50.25	11.4	63.75
516–660	6.0	67.04	5.2	62.17	9.3	78.72
660–900	3.7	86.94	2.8	81.88	7.6	94.90
900 and above	2.8	134.60	1.9	130.78	6.9	139.00
All classes	100.0	38.35	100.0	34.31	100.0	55.48
Average expenditure, all classes		344		322		438

Source: Government of India, Cabinet Secretariat, *The National Sample Survey*, 19th Round: July 1964–June 1965 (Delhi: Manager of Publications, 1972).

Table A-5. *Expenditure per Capita on Dairy Products, Meat, Eggs, and Fish, by Expenditure Class, India, 1964–65*

Amounts in rupees per year

Expenditure class	Total population		Rural population		Urban population	
	Percent in class	Expenditure	Percent in class	Expenditure	Percent in class	Expenditure
0–96	1.3	2.27	1.5	2.31	0.5	1.82
96–132	4.6	4.65	5.1	4.50	2.3	6.08
132–156	5.2	6.32	5.8	5.84	3.0	10.22
156–180	6.8	9.00	7.3	8.64	4.9	11.31
180–216	11.6	11.32	12.1	10.58	9.4	15.33
216–252	12.3	17.34	12.8	16.42	10.0	22.39
252–288	11.2	23.89	11.6	22.75	9.7	29.68
288–336	11.8	29.77	11.8	28.35	11.5	35.89
336–408	12.7	40.37	12.5	38.81	13.6	46.48
408–516	10.0	55.01	9.6	52.68	11.4	63.39
516–660	6.0	77.01	5.2	73.36	9.2	85.77
660–900	3.7	106.83	2.8	103.05	7.6	112.78
900 and above	2.8	157.85	1.9	136.92	6.9	181.94
All classes	100.0	34.48	100.0	29.81	100.0	54.26
Average expenditure, all classes		344		322		438

Source: Same as table A-4.

Table A-6. *Population, by Expenditure Class, India, 1964–65*

Expenditure class (rupees per year)	Population (millions)			Percent of total	
	Rural	Urban	Total	Rural	Urban
0–96	5.98	0.50	6.48	92.3	7.7
96–132	19.98	2.11	22.09	90.4	9.6
132–156	22.52	2.76	25.28	89.1	10.9
156–180	28.39	4.50	32.89	86.3	13.7
180–216	47.19	8.66	55.85	84.5	15.5
216–252	50.20	9.18	59.38	84.5	15.5
252–288	45.39	8.91	54.30	83.6	16.4
288–336	46.23	10.61	56.84	81.3	18.7
336–408	48.72	12.47	61.19	79.6	20.4
408–516	37.65	10.47	48.12	78.2	21.8
516–660	20.49	8.52	29.01	70.6	29.4
660–900	10.99	6.95	17.94	61.3	38.7
900 and above	7.27	6.35	13.62	53.4	46.6
All classes	391	92	483	81.0	19.0

Source: Estimates based on percentages in Government of India, Cabinet Secretariat, *The National Sample Survey, Tables with Notes on Consumer Expenditure*, 19th Round: July 1964–June 1965, no. 192 (Delhi: Manager of Publications, 1972), table 1.3.0, pp. 18–20; table 2.3.0, pp. 60–62.

Figure A-1. *Rainfall Indexes and Yield, Various Crops, India,*
1951–52 to 1977–78

Percentage of twenty-year average rainfall, 1957–58 to 1976–77

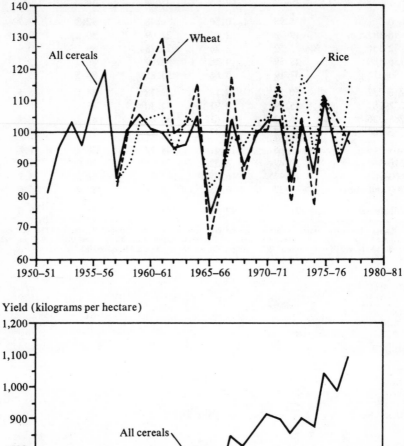

Yield (kilograms per hectare)

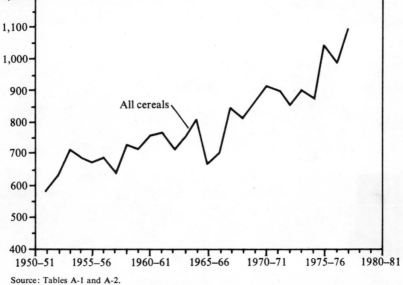

Source: Tables A-1 and A-2.